Freedom and Obligation

Also by C. K. Barrett and published by SPCK

The Gospel According to St John
The Gospel of John and Judaism
Essays on Paul
Essays on John

C. K. BARRETT

Freedom and Obligation

A Study of the
Epistle to the Galatians

First published in Great Britain 1985
SPCK
Holy Trinity Church
Marylebone Road
London NW1 4DU

British Library Cataloguing in Publication Data

Barrett, C. K.
 Freedom and obligation: a study of the Epistle to the Galatians.
 1. Bible. N.T. Galatians—Commentaries
 I. Title
 227'.406   BS2685.3
 ISBN 0-281-04149-0

Printed in Great Britain by
Eyre & Spottiswoode Ltd, Thanet Press, Margate

Contents

Preface

This book contains the Sanderson Lectures, given in the Theological Hall of the Uniting Church of Australia, within the United Faculty of Theology at Melbourne, in March and April 1983. My first task in this Preface, a duty and at least equally a pleasure, is to thank those who invited me to give the lectures, and all those whose hospitality and friendship made the term we spent in Ormond College an unforgettable happiness for both my wife and myself. After some thought I have decided to print the lectures as they were delivered, with the restoration of a number of paragraphs which I was obliged to omit because I had prepared more than could be accommodated in the time allotted for delivery, and the addition of a few notes which for various reasons seemed called for. I was asked to give lectures which could be understood not only by theologians but also by intelligent listeners without technical theological equipment. Readers who belong to the latter category may ignore the notes completely; professionals may wish to have a few references. I do not regret the brevity that results from this procedure. If I were to write more I could not stop short of a full-dress commentary, and that is something I have no time to write; nor should I wish to compete with the recent masterly commentary by Professor H. D. Betz.

In the first lecture I have said something of my desire to write and lecture on a subject related to the Epistle to the Galatians. I should like to add here a reference to another volume of lectures based on Galatians: W. M. Macgregor's Baird Lectures (1913), *Christian Freedom* (London 1914, 2nd edn 1931), a book that ought to be far better known than it is. I hoped at first that I might be able to produce an equivalent course of lectures, seventy years on; but for this I had neither the time nor, I fear, the ability.

The five Sanderson Lectures were compressed into three West Watson Lectures at Christchurch, New Zealand; selections were given at other places in Australia and New Zealand, and I have often spoken about the Epistle to the Galatians in recent years, thinking my way through as I went. I am grateful to many hearers for their kindness and their contributions. They cannot, unfortunately, be mentioned by name any more than I can refer to all the important books I have consulted.

vii

To the Australian lectures I have added 'Apostles in Council and in Conflict', the Henton Davies Lecture given at Regents Park College, Oxford, in February 1983. It handles a related topic, and this seemed a convenient place in which to print it. I gladly take this opportunity of saluting an old friend, once a Durham colleague.

Durham, September 1983   C. K. BARRETT

ONE

The Story of a Struggle

Freedom and obligation are terms, concepts, facts – it is hard to know the right word to use at this point – in regard to which our generation has not been particularly successful. It is certainly true that freedom, at least as a slogan, has enjoyed great popularity, much greater popularity than obligation. Indeed, freedom, with its concomitant democracy, has been one of the most popular of watchwords; one of the most popular, and one of the most abused, often most highly lauded in places where its practice has been most radically denied. It is all the more important to attend to the relation between the two: freedom, and obligation. Freedom is a concept that calls for wholeness. I am not a fully free member of society if I am restricted whether politically or economically, and I am not a fully free person if I am not a member of a fully free society, if, that is, I exercise my freedom at the expense of others. This means that freedom, true freedom, is always and necessarily accompanied by obligation, a term as unpopular as freedom is popular – that is, when it is applied to myself. As the common saying, which few avow but many practise, runs, 'The world owes me a living'; the obligation of others to me, but not of me to others, is allowed. Even the much used phrase, 'the right to work', is often used in the sense of, 'my right to an agreeable and suitably rewarded occupation: the obligation of society to me'. Of course, I am looking on the dark side, and anyone could cite noble and shining examples of a very different frame of mind. But I am not inventing anything; in any case, it is truly difficult to hold freedom and obligation together, whether philosophically or practically; I shall not blame others for failing to achieve what I cannot very successfully manage myself.

I have been speaking of the world at large. It is a more serious matter that the same failure to combine freedom and obligation has marked the life of the Church. It is true (as it ought to be) that Christians have seldom failed to recognize that their life, individually and corporately, should be marked by both characteristics. But (and again I omit to mention exceptions that all could supply) they have too often mixed them up, and imposed obligation in areas where there should have been freedom, and allowed freedom to reign where obligation was called for. No-one reading the theological literature and observing the ecclesiastical politics of the last three decades can fail to observe a loosening of the claims of doctrine and morality, and a readiness both to insist upon and to grant a tightening of the institutional bonds of church life. Whether this is a true or an inverted understanding of Christian freedom and of Christian obligation may appear as we proceed.

That statement leads me to my subtitle. There are those who could discuss for your instruction the nature and the interrelation of freedom and obligation as philosophical concepts. This is a task quite beyond my ability; if I am to examine the theme at all it must be by a different method, or methods – those of exegesis and of history. In the realm of Christian theology, which rests upon a historical event, attested and given its first and classical interpretation in certain texts, now ancient and written in a language not universally known or even very widely studied, this is anything but excuse-making; the exegete has rights prior to those of the philosopher, and so has the historian. And the Epistle to the Galatians needs apology no more than it needs introduction. I must admit a personal interest here. I spent perhaps the best twenty years of my life, and used such skill and understanding as I could muster, in writing commentaries on Romans, and on 1 and 2 Corinthians. With these, Galatians forms the fourth *Hauptbrief*, or chief epistle, and I have long wished, not to write a full-dress commentary on Galatians, but in some other way to expound its message. The four are rightly described as *Hauptbriefe*; not in the sense of authorship, though indeed they do not evoke the niggling sense of doubt that may inhibit the use of, say, Colossians or 2 Thessalonians, but in the far more important sense, which is open to no doubt whatever, that nearly everything truly characteristic of Paul's theology is contained in them. Remove the rest and we should still know and sit at the feet of the great *Doctor Gentium*; remove these, and Paulinism would be emasculated, indeed would scarcely exist.

I am not however inflicting upon you a merely personal whim. 'The Epistle to the Galatians', said Luther, 'is my epistle; I have betrothed myself to it; it is my wife.' It was, if one may put it so, a fruitful marriage; and I am not thinking only of the prolixity which Luther himself acknowledged in his later exposition. As H. D. Betz[1] was to say in 1979, the book is 'more than a scholarly commentary *upon* Galatians. It is a recreation *of* Galatians in the sixteenth century. Luther speaks as Paul would have spoken had

2

he lived at the time when Luther gave his lectures.' The moral of that might seem to be: Cut these lectures and read Luther's Commentary instead! Yet not so, for this is not the sixteenth century but the twentieth, and though we should learn from Luther as from other expositors of the past we cannot, or should not, simply repeat his words. We may however proceed from the same starting-point. When Luther wrote at the beginning of his booklet on Christian freedom,[2] *'Eyn Christen mensch ist eyn freyer herr über alle ding und niemandt unterthan. Eyn Christen mensch ist eyn dienstpar knecht aller ding und ydermann unterthan'* (A Christian man is the most free lord of all, and subject to none; a Christian man is the most dutiful servant of all, and subject to everyone), he turned almost immediately to Galatians, referring in the next few lines to 1 Corinthians 9.19; Romans 13.8; and Galatians 4.4; and there is none even among the Pauline letters that so boldly and firmly clamps together *freyheit* and *dienstparkeit* as Galatians. I am very far from claiming that we shall in these few lectures solve all the problems of freedom and obligation; but I believe we are beginning our search for answers in the right place.

At this point it remains only to sketch in advance the way in which the inquiry is to be conducted. More neatly and equally than most sermons the epistle falls into three clearly defined parts. Paul's first step in dealing with the troubled situation in his Galatian churches is to set straight the record of the past; till that is done there can be no hope of securing the future. Thus the first two chapters could be headed 'History'. Having set out the facts of the past Paul proceeds to lay the theological foundation upon which the future must rest; and chapters 3 and 4 could be headed 'Theology' – a theology of freedom. Right thinking calls for corresponding right action and the next chapters, 5 and 6, we may entitle 'Ethics' – ethics of obligation. I need not point out that this is a very broad division and that the several themes interpenetrate each other. The epistle is a unity, and this unity of diverse elements is one of the most characteristic and important features of it. There are plenty of theological hints in chapters 1 and 2; in chapter 4 there is a considerable paragraph of history; chapters 5 and 6 are theological through and through and their ethical teaching is closely related to the situation in Galatia. The interrelation, interpenetration of history and theology is, I have said, specially characteristic of Galatians, but it is a distinctive feature of New Testament theology as a whole, of which Galatians provides a particularly striking example, lacking, it may be, the depth and range of Romans but even more alive because nearer to the heat of controversy in which Paul's theology was forged. In the study of the New Testament it is a prime error to separate the three strands of history, theology and ethics. New Testament history is theological history; I mean not simply that historical events were seen to be theologically significant but that they were theologically motivated. Certainly they were conditioned by a variety of sociological factors, but the theological factor was usually (it would be wrong to say always) dominant. It follows that the theology of the New Testament is bound up with history. It is doubtful whether any New Testament writer (even the Fourth Evangelist) simply sat down in a speculative mood and evolved theological propositions for the love of doing so. Certainly Paul did not do so. He had to fight, inwardly and outwardly, for the theology he achieved, and he had to fight for the freedom of the gospel as he understood it. This, as I hinted a moment ago, explains the vitality and importance of Galatians, which stands at the heart of the New Testament. This is so historically, because Paul's conflicts with Judaism and with Jewish Christianity ensured the freedom of the gospel to generate a potentially universal Church, and it is so theologically because the same conflicts provided a channel for the life and teaching of Jesus to flow through the ages, as the centrality and sufficiency of grace are affirmed. These conflicts, so far from removing Galatians to the periphery of the New Testament, as some think, set the epistle firmly at its centre.

History and theology, then, belong together; as for ethics, it is, as Barth said,[3] the doctrine of the command of God, and is thus closely related to theology, perhaps we should say, it is the historical manifestation of theological truth. But that anticipates conclusions regarding freedom and obligation.

To be practical: I shall spend the rest of this chapter on the historical events presupposed by the letter, with some inevitable glances at the theological issues involved. We shall have in mind mainly chapters 1 and 2 of Galatians. In the second and third chapters we shall be concerned mainly with chapters 3 and 4 of the epistle, and I shall try to approach Paul's theology by asking first what the theology was that he opposed, and on what this theology was based. In the fourth and fifth chapters our exegetical base will be Galatians 5 and 6, and we shall work through the contrast of flesh and spirit to Paul's final working out of the relation between history, theology and ethics, and should be able to draw some

conclusions regarding the theme which I have already set out.
What then are we to say under the heading of history? Where
are we to look and what are we to look for? There are two sources
that we may use, and neither of them is entirely satisfactory. One,
of course, is Galatians. I have said that this epistle is central in the
history of the first Christian generation, and so it is; this does not
make it a satisfactory historical source. It is unsatisfactory not
because it is false but because it is personal, and therefore partial
and one-sided. It was never intended to be a comprehensive judicial statement of all the facts. A number of the facts Paul can
simply omit because he knows that his readers know them as well
as he does; others, important in their own way, especially in
respect of order and chronology, he omits because they do not
bear upon the case he is concerned to make. The second source is
Acts. This too is unsatisfactory, for two reasons. Luke, like Paul,
had no intention of describing every single thing that happened –
even in his time Christendom was wider than Galatia, and there
were other things to write about. And, unlike Paul, he wrote at
some considerable distance from the events in question. This does
not mean, as some think, that Luke can be simply written off as
a historian. He was not nefariously whitewashing the first Christians, so that we cannot trust him; he is using traditional material
for the edification of the Church of his own time. What he judges
will not serve that end he omits. If I may offer a comparison, it
is as if I were to sit down to write, without reference books, and
with the intention of bringing certain truths home to Christians
in the 1980s, a brief sketch of the Confessing Church in Germany
under Hitler. This is a subject that has fascinated me since the late
1930s; I have read a fair amount about it; I know a number of
people who were involved in it. A sketch written by me might
do some justice to the main principles that were at stake and the
broad lines on which events developed; it would evince great
admiration for some of the people concerned; it would contain a
few interesting and moving anecdotes; it might even do its readers
some good. But it would contain errors, and it would be far from
complete. Acts is something like this; and the result is that we shall
never have a complete account of the history that lies behind
Galatians – and I need not add that if we had such an account it
could not be compressed into one lecture. Since the evidence is
incomplete different students will make different guesses to fill the
gaps, and these different guesses will lead them to give different
interpretations of the evidence we do have.

Enough of excuses. Let us see what we can do. Since I must be selective I shall avoid as far as possible the familiar questions that some of us had to get up in our first year's study of Theology – Was the epistle written early in Paul's career, or in the middle period, along with Romans and the Corinthian letters? What did Paul mean by Galatia? – the area in north central Asia Minor occupied by the ancient Gallic kingdom, or the more southerly territory added to the old kingdom when the Romans made a province of it?[4] These old questions have their importance not because it matters much where we write the name Galatia on the map but because it matters a great deal whether the Judaizing movement, the opposition to Paul, sprang up quickly as the result of an honest mistake on the part of good men, and was as quickly ended, or was the work of a convinced and organized anti-Pauline party, prepared to go to any lengths to destroy the apostle's work. This is in fact just the kind of significant historical question that is inseparable from theology and therefore of contemporary relevance, for the divisions and controversies of the first Christian generation are not unrelated to those of our own.

The historical questions that I have in mind can be divided into four groups: those related specifically to Paul's own career, those related to Jerusalem, to Antioch, and to Galatia. These are all indeed related to one another; it is precisely because Paul thought they were related that he discusses the troubles of Galatia in terms of what happened in Jerusalem and Antioch. His concern throughout is practical, and neither historical nor even autobiographical. Yet the various areas – thematic and geographical – should not be confused. It must not be assumed that the same issues arose in the same form in each geographical location. It seems almost certain that, notwithstanding a close relationship, this was not so and that this fact was responsible for a good deal of the difficulty Paul evidently found in communicating with his churches. This variety is important because it makes it more natural and proper for us to apply Paul's principles to our own – also different, yet related – circumstances. This however is no excuse for cutting the historical investigation; it makes it all the more essential. I hope to pursue it in greater detail elsewhere; here I am being – like Paul – selective and allusive. We are to see freedom and obligation threatened and vindicated.

Under the first heading of Paul's personal affairs there are three matters that we must consider: conversion, apostleship and tradition.

Acts tells more vividly than Paul the transformation of the zealous persecutor into the equally zealous preacher of the faith, and indeed tells it three times. Luke was not greatly concerned with the details, except to use them to give life to his narrative, for he does not trouble to make his three accounts fully consistent with one another. There is however a significant agreement between Acts and Paul's own narrative. Not only does Paul confirm his activity in anti-Christian propaganda and persecution, like Luke he makes it clear that the decisive event was a meeting between himself and Jesus, a person hitherto supposed dead. There is no record of a psychological disentanglement, only of the conviction that the crucified Jesus was now alive and at work. Romans 7 has misled many on this point; the record is: 'It pleased him who separated me from my mother's womb and called me through his grace to reveal his Son to me' (Galatians 1.15). This, it is true, was a more revolutionary event than any psychological operation could have been, for it meant that Paul was at once set free and obliged, not indeed to abandon all his Jewish presuppositions, but to rethink and reorientate them; this happened not only in regard to law (as we may see throughout the epistle) and in regard to eschatology, (so for example Galatians 1.4: deliverance from the present evil age is already afoot).[5] The basis of the whole theological revolution however was the simple conviction that Jesus was alive. Hidden behind Paul's account of this lies a problem, which comes to light in 1 Corinthians 15.8. There Paul claims the appearance of Jesus to him as a resurrection appearance; but it came very late – so late that Paul could be called a freak, and thought of by some as no apostle at all. Acts places the conversion appearance after the ascension, and thus classes it with the appearance to Stephen in Acts 7.55 and the later appearance to Paul in 23.11. This may have contributed to Luke's unwillingness to describe Paul as an apostle.[6]

This provides us with a cue for moving on to the second point, for, whatever view others may have taken, Paul was in no doubt of his apostleship. This was given him in and with his conversion. The appearance of Jesus not only made a Christian of him, it made him an apostle. 'God ... revealed his Son to me that I might preach him among the Gentiles' (1.16). True, he did not meet the requirements laid down in Acts 1.21f.; he had not been a companion of Jesus' during Jesus' earthly ministry, and he had not (or it could be maintained that he had not) seen the risen Jesus in the same sense that Peter and James, for example, had seen him.

7

This did not worry Paul. At the beginning of the epistle he describes himself as 'an apostle not from men or through man but through Jesus Christ and God ... who raised him from the dead' (1.1), and one of the main themes of the epistle is his independence of the authorities in Jerusalem or elsewhere. It was God who made his Gentile mission possible (2.8, ἐνήργησεν), and the theme of freedom is encountered first in the freedom of God, part of whose freedom to act in grace is expressed in the freedom to find and make apostles where he wills, even where the customary qualifications are lacking. The same freedom is expressed in 1.15 (it pleased God to reveal his Son), and again in Paul's reaction to his vocation (which recalls those of the prophets):[7] 'The first thing I did was not to confer with flesh and blood, or to go up to Jerusalem to those who where apostles before me, but I went off into Arabia' (1.16f.). When God speaks, man acts – God's freedom, man's obligation. The negative side of Paul's response simply underlines what I have already said. When God commands, what need to go to Jerusalem? What can Jerusalem give that God cannot? The positive side probably means not that Paul went off into the Arabian desert for a period of meditation but that he immediately began a mission to the Arabs, beginning at once to obey the command to preach Christ amongst the Gentiles. There is some confirmation of this in the incident recorded in 2 Corinthians 11.32f. – Paul had begun as he undoubtedly continued, and had made himself such a nuisance in Arabia that Aretas, king of the Nabataean Arabs, set his ethnarch to chase him out of Damascus.

It is not surprising that Paul's apostleship was questioned. It was not only resentment at the rise of an upstart that evoked a jealous, defensive reaction. It could be, no doubt was, argued that Christianity began from Jerusalem; that was where Jesus had died and risen from the dead, that was where his first followers were to be found. If anyone knew what Christianity was, and was authorized to proclaim it, it was they. If Paul agreed with them, he was dependent on them, at best a secondary authority; if he disagreed with them, so much the worse for him – he must be wrong. There is truth in this attitude. A Christianity that is divorced from Jesus crucified and risen is not Christianity at all, and a defence based on the bare assertion of God's freedom to find and call apostles where he chooses is one that calls for very delicate handling. Paul is at pains not to represent himself as a cantankerous free-lance. He had been made an apostle by Jesus and the word, but when the opportunity arose, after three years he went up to Jerusalem to visit Peter. He was satisfied that God had made Peter too an apostle (2.8). But here too the stress lies in Paul's independence. What are fifteen days in fifteen or sixteen years (1.18; 2.1)?[8] His contacts with Jerusalem were exiguous. He was a missionary in his own right and the Judaean Christians rejoiced in the fact (1.22–4).

It is here that the third point I have mentioned must be considered. You cannot be a missionary unless you have something to say; how did Paul know what to say? What was his relation to the earlier Christian tradition? A quick reading of Galatians 1 might suggest the answer: None. 'The gospel that was preached by me is not according to man, for neither did I receive it from man, nor was I taught it, but it came through a revelation of Jesus Christ' (1.11f.).[9] But what does Paul mean by this? He must already have known a good deal of the content of Christian belief when he was persecuting the Church; he was no fool, and would not have wasted time and energy in persecuting a group with which he had no quarrel. He knew what they believed; he learnt it from them when they were his enemies. Elsewhere he stresses his agreement with those who were Christians before him. 'I handed on to you that which also I received' (1 Cor.15.3). There follows the basic outline not of theology but of the facts on which Christian theology rests: Christ died for our sins, he was buried, the third day he was raised from the dead. And the paragraph concludes with the words, 'Whether then it be I or they, so we preach and so you believed' (15.11). The same propositions are echoed in Galatians 1.4. There is no contradiction here. The question that was settled by Paul's conversion was not what Christians believed, but whether what Christians believed was true; and it was settled not by a paper proof but by the personal appearance of the central character. This is not to say that the beliefs of Paul, Peter and James were identical; that is a question to which we shall return. For the moment I turn aside to note the unreal conflict that is sometimes whipped up between inspiration and tradition. It is unreal because both these elements are needed and they should not conflict. It is only through the corporate memory of the Church (now preserved in Scripture) that we know the facts about Jesus, but it is not on the authority of this corporate memory that we know Jesus as Lord and that God raised him from the dead. Here is an obligation freely accepted by men set free by God; and if a man does not know this for himself he does not know it at all.

So much then for the early part of Paul's story, which introduces us to the themes of conversion, apostleship and tradition. The rest of his story is taken up in the remaining divisions of our historical sketch.

I have already mentioned Paul's visit to Jerusalem when he stayed with Cephas and also met James – no other apostle.[10] Fourteen years later he was there again. Here we encounter the most celebrated and complicated historical problem in the whole epistle – perhaps in the whole of the New Testament. The most difficult question I shall mention and pass on; there is no time to deal with it: How can we co-ordinate Paul's movements as narrated by himself with the story as told in Acts? According to Galatians, Paul's stay with Cephas was Jerusalem Visit 1; his later visit, described in Galatians 2, was Jerusalem Visit 2. In Acts, Paul visits Jerusalem soon after his conversion (Acts 9); again, in order to convey relief to the poor (Acts 11, 12); and then a third time because people come to Antioch and say that Gentiles cannot be saved unless they are circumcised and keep the law of Moses (Acts 15). With which of these does Galatians 2 correspond? A fascinating problem, but it is one for a lecture on Acts. If there is any discrepancy and we have to choose, we must follow Paul.[11] Paul certainly knew what happened, and even if he had not been a truthful man it would, in a controversial setting, have been suicidal for him to leave anything out or make false statements. His enemies would have picked on them at once: 'He never mentioned that visit to Jerusalem! That was when he made his submission to the great apostles and received his subordinate status from them.' I am not saying that we have nothing to learn from Acts; I am saying that our time is limited and that we shall, if we are wise, stick to the source we know to be first-hand.

Not that Galatians 2 presents no problems; it bristles with them. Paul went up to Jerusalem by revelation (2.2). Perhaps the negative aspect of this is what he wants to draw out here: he did not go because he was sent for. There was no carpeting of a wayward subordinate by the great men. He went of his own volition; better, he went because God told him to. Barnabas, a Jew, and Titus, a Gentile, were with him (2.1). Why? Because he needed friends; but the racial mix can hardly have been an accident. Now, after sixteen years or so, Paul put before the authorities (not all and sundry) the gospel he preached in the Gentile world. Again, why? It would not make sense that after so long he should develop cold feet and wonder if what he was preaching, the message that had converted men and women, changed their lives, and gathered them into churches, was perhaps a mistake. He does not say that he was seeking either correction or validation. It is nearer the truth to say that he could see that trouble was blowing up (the next few verses will show how near it was), and went to lay his cards on the table, recognizing that though the Jerusalem authorities could not prove him wrong or right they could ruin his life's work (2.2). Perhaps what he wanted was a show-down, and he took Titus with him as a deliberate provocation. Jerusalem was evidently a divided church, for we leave the authorities and come first to the false brothers (2.4), that is, people who looked like Christians, and claimed to be Christians, but (in Paul's view) were not Christians. It was these men who required that Titus, the Greek, should be circumcised, evidently taking the line that this was the only way into the Christian body, the people of God. Paul would not have it. There are notorious textual problems here, and I do not intend to discuss them.[12] Some think that Titus was circumcised though he was not compelled to be circumcised; there is even the view that Titus went off and had himself circumcised without Paul's knowledge, and to Paul's confusion and embarrassment. I do not agree with either of these views, but it is enough for the present to note that the false brothers wanted to compel Titus to be circumcised, and failed to carry the day. What did they really want? To 'spy out our liberty' (2.4); but did they not already know it without the use of secret service methods? I think Paul lays the stress on 'bringing us into bondage' (2.4), and that 'spying' refers to underhand methods, not precisely defined. This means that there was in Jerusalem a group of men, calling themselves Christians (though Paul believed they did not deserve the title), who thought it right that Greek converts to Christianity should be circumcised, did not believe in what Paul regarded as Christian liberty, and adopted underhand means to destroy it. But Paul did not yield to them, nor did they get the support they may have expected from those leading figures who bore the title 'pillars' (2.6, 9).[13] These men, on the contrary, recognized Paul's position. So much is clear; it is not clear what the recognition meant. 'They contributed nothing to me';[14] does this mean that they added no doctrines (such as the indispensability of circumcision) to what Paul taught, or that they conferred on him no new authority that he did not already possess? The former alternative is often assumed in view of verse 2, but this is a long way back, and it may be better to look forward to verses 7, 8. Two pairs of parallel propositions are made here. In verse 7, it is said that Paul has been entrusted with the gospel of the uncircumcision, Peter with the gospel of the circumcision. In verse 8, it is said that God has created for Peter an apostolate of the circumcision, and for Paul has acted similarly (is it by accident only that the word ἀποστολή is not repeated?)[15] with regard to the uncircumcision. It naturally follows in verse 9 that the 'pillar' apostles are to go to the circumcision, Paul and Barnabas to the Gentiles. What does this agreement mean? It appears to mean that there are two gospels and two apostolates; but perhaps it is an awkward way of saying that though there is only one gospel it is bound to take different forms as it is presented to different hearers, that though there is only one apostolate different apostles will go in different directions and evangelize different groups. The obscurity and ambiguity of the language are a pointer to the fact that what agreement there was had probably been inadequately thought through. In view of verse 9 it seems probable that what was in mind throughout was a division of labour. Paul, as an apostle, or quasi-apostle, would carry the gospel to the Gentiles; Peter and his colleagues, as apostles, would carry the gospel to the Jews, each group formulating its message in what seemed appropriate terms. There was some agreement, there was common ground; but F. C. Baur was right when he said that the agreement was only superficial.[16] Lurking beneath the surface was an underlying disagreement, a radical understanding of the gospel on Paul's part which was not shared by his colleagues in Jerusalem. What this was we shall see shortly, and understand more fully as we deal with the more explicitly theological parts of the epistle. For the present, we press on with the history, noting in confirmation of what I have just said the delicate irony of the reference to those who thought of themselves as 'pillars' and the scarcely concealed antipathy of 'Whatever they were makes no difference to me; God does not judge by appearance' (2.9, 6).

We move on to a new scene, in Antioch; and the first glimpse is a pleasing one. Here is a mixed church, composed of Jews and Gentiles, led respectively by Peter and Paul, and all live together in unity. Peter the Jew, with his Jewish colleagues, eats with his Gentile Christian brethren. This common eating will have included the common Christian meal, the Lord's Supper, or Eucharist, if that is not an anachronistic term. They have not noticed that they are in a situation which the Jerusalem discussion had not contemplated, but it is not long before a reminder comes from Jerusalem (2.12). We may reconstruct its content. 'We agreed that

Gentiles might be evangelized, and that they might be converted and baptized; we allowed that they did not have to be circumcised, but we never said that they might be permitted to share meals with Jews. They are Christians, but not Christians who can be allowed to share our Eucharist.' Those who said this came from James, and presumably Paul, rightly or wrongly, understood that they represented the mind of James. If this belief is to be taken seriously it means that there were at this time several distinct groups of Christians whose views covered a wide range. At one extreme were the bogus Christians, as Paul regards them, who believed that to be a Christian one had to become in all respects a Jew. Paul's programme of Christian freedom was wrong, they thought, and should be stopped. Christianity was a new version of Jewish legal obligation. Next came James, who believed that there was a proper Christian mission to Gentiles, and that in order to be saved it was not necessary to be circumcised and live in accordance with the law. But that was all; James had probably not contemplated the existence of mixed churches, and when he heard that there was one in Antioch he reacted with horror to the notion that Jews should so far relax their legal observance as to eat with Gentiles. What he required was evidently withdrawal; not an unchurching of Gentiles, but a separation of the Jewish church (the church of obligation) from the Gentile church (the church of freedom). His message to Peter was couched in such terms that Peter knew he must obey. We can hardly speak of a distinct Petrine position, for Peter seems to have adopted the line of the strongest adjacent force; but it is worth noticing that for him (and Barnabas and the other Jews) the absent James was a more powerful influence than the present Paul. Peter was a Palestinian Jew, a Galilean Jew whose attitude had been changed by his knowledge of Jesus. He lacked however the solidity of purpose to stand up to determined opposition. Perhaps we should say that what he lacked was theology; a consistent theology would have led to consistent action. He is a warning to the minister who thinks he can do without theology. Paul's own position was clear. Christ was the end of the law, and this meant, among other things, that it was no longer legal regulations but Christ – Christ who had been notorious for eating with publicans and sinners – who governed the terms on which men were related to one another. 'Receive one another', Paul wrote to the Romans (15.7), 'as Christ received you.' There is still no better precept for inter-church relations. Summary descriptions are always dangerous, but it will not be misleading to say that the false brothers stood for the law, with a certain respect for Jesus; James stood for Jesus and the law, at least for Jews; Paul stood for Jesus only. The result shows the power of legalism, for James's attempt to combine the two clearly resulted in the victory of legalism – so at least Paul believed: and his own extreme line was (from the Christian point of view) the only safe one. Freedom must be established first, and in the gracious freedom of God. Freedom and obligation may turn out to be a tolerable combination, but 'obligation first and freedom as a reward' would never suit Paul. We shall see as we proceed that the whole theological development of Galatians is a working out of the principle of 'Jesus only' against the counter-principle of 'Jesus and . . .'.

We come finally to the fourth circle of historical problems, those touching Galatia itself. These are the most difficult to unravel. Paul had to tell the Galatians what had happened in Jerusalem, for they had no more been present there than we, and the account Paul thought would suffice for them is not totally inadequate for us. The same is true of Antioch. But Paul was under no necessity to tell his readers what had happened on their own doorstep: they knew as well as he – perhaps better – and allusions would therefore suffice. They do not suffice for us, and we have to fill in the gaps with a good deal of guessing. It is clear that, in the beginning, Paul had been received with great, with surprising enthusiasm, as if he had been an angel, as if he had been Christ himself (4.12–15). In his absence, however, things had gone badly wrong, not, it seems, through internal stress but, as in Corinth, through men who came into the Church from without. It is not easy to put together all the shreds of evidence. The warm welcome had gone sour (4.16–20) on account of people who had come and paid court to the Galatians, apparently seeking to win their loyalty and affection, thereby separating them from Paul and from Paul's gospel. In chapter 4 this alienation is described in personal terms; the theological counterpart to this paragraph occurs in 3.1–5; we shall attend to this later (pp. 21, 22). In 1.6–8 we hear of 'those who are troubling you', by seeking your attachment to a different gospel, different from mine – only it is in fact no gospel, no good news, at all. At 5.12 we hear of 'those' [plural] 'who are upsetting you' and at 5.10 of 'he' [singular] 'who is troubling you'. In 6.12, 13 it becomes clear that though other matters are involved (4.10) circumcision is at the heart of the dispute. So troublers have come to Galatia; there is one troubler in particular. There is then a party with a ringleader. The party corresponds in its interests with the false brothers of 2.4; is it possible that 'the troubler' is James, whom Paul will not name (cf. 2 Corinthians 10.10f.) because he hopes that he is still in at least partial agreement? Paul may have intended that the Galatians should recognize their own trouble-makers in those who came to Antioch from James (2.12); certainly his account of his stand against Peter on this occasion leads straight into the argument of Galatians as a whole. Whatever the relation of the Galatian intruders to James may have been they had the effect of showing that James's compromise would not work. This mediating position claims that Christ alone is sufficient for salvation, but if you wish to be fully a member of the visible people of God you must be circumcised and keep the law. But has being a member of the people of God nothing to do with being saved? And is it tolerable that there should exist two groups, both 'saved' but out of communion with each other? Paul and the all-out Judaizers agree in this if in nothing else, that they both answer that question No. There can be only one saved people of God. The latter drew the conclusion that, since some members of the people of God are already circumcised, and since the old regulations for the first phase of the People's existence require circumcision, and since further it is unthinkable that God's people should not live in obedience to him, all members must, as a necessary condition of membership, be circumcised. Let them by all means believe in Jesus as the Christ, but let them not seek to avoid their legal obligation. Over against this view, and as the only logical alternative to it, Paul says, 'if righteousness is achieved through the law, Christ might as well not have died' (2.21) – an absurd conclusion, so that the premise must be mistaken. Righteousness is not through the law but through Christ alone. Two propositions follow: circumcision is nothing, uncircumcision is nothing; it is neither the one nor the other that makes a Christian, but a new act of creation (6.15). But since this is so, if you, being an uncircumcised Christian, get yourself circumcised, you have finished with Christ, you have fallen out of grace (5.2, 4).[17]

We are already on the fringe of the theology which is the proper theme of the next two chapters. All that we must observe at the present time is that interpenetration of history and theology that I have already mentioned.[18] Paul is contending for the Christian freedom to which his Galatian converts have been introduced, but he does so not in the name of humane liberalism, but on the basis of a radical theological understanding of the gospel. It is already clear that if he believed that any obligation lies upon Christians it will not be a legal obligation; its foundation and sanction will have to be found elsewhere. The only purely historical question we may ask at this point is, What happened next in Galatia? What was the effect of Paul's letter? The plain disappointing fact is that we do not know. Evidently when the Galatians received the letter they did not immediately rip up the papyrus in anger. But was it preserved, venerated, acted on, by the whole church? or was it rescued, hidden, and kept for posterity by a small minority who held fast to the Pauline gospel while the rest fell away? 1 Peter suggests that when it was written a substantially Pauline Christianity was still to be found in Galatia, along with Pontus, Cappadocia, Asia, and Bithynia (1 Peter 1.1). The outcome – in Jerusalem and Antioch too – is for us less important than Paul's clarification of the issues involved in the conflict.

For the historian it is also important to see the great variety of outlook that existed in the early decades of the Church's life, and the violence of controversy that flared up between the several parties. We should not conclude that such bitterness is a normal and necessary constituent of Christian existence, but it should prevent us from romanticizing those idyllic days of the undivided apostolic Church. It is important too to see that though no side abstained on principle from personalities the matters that were fought over were theological matters of permanent importance. In the discussion of these matters Peter serves as the outstanding example of the man without a theological foundation, without a theological backbone, who in consequence is blown along by any wind of doctrine that springs up. He was in a difficult position because as yet there was no accepted orthodoxy. Orthodoxy had not yet come into being; even Paul has little idea of it. Perhaps wisely he has no credal formulas cast in metaphysical terms; but he fights tooth and nail, with the blast of anathemas, for a Christ-centred gospel, which constitutes at once the freedom and the obligation of a Christian man. But this is theology, and must be kept for further chapters.

TWO

The Theology of Freedom:
The Debate

The key-word of the last chapter was history, and we traced Paul's account of his own career and of events in Jerusalem, Antioch and Galatia. But our study of these events will, I hope, have justified my initial assertion that in Galatians, to an even greater extent than in the New Testament as a whole, history is inseparable from theology, theology from history, so that if I say that in the present chapter we are turning to theology this does not mean that we are leaving history for something totally different. The inter-penetration of history, theology and ethics, this rather than any one of the three, is my fundamental topic, and the relation between freedom and obligation is to be discovered, if discovered at all, in theology, expressed in ethics and manifested on the field of history.

More explicitly and simply we considered Paul's conversion and call to be an apostle; the struggle against freedom in Jerusalem, and Paul's victory in the cause of liberty; the failure in Antioch; and the fact that in Galatia, whatever precisely may have been afoot, things were going so badly that Paul feared he might after all have run in vain. There were, as we know from other letters, similar troubles elsewhere. The gospel was perverted, the churches were corrupted. Paul's first reaction was, as I have said, to turn to history. 'Let us set the record straight, and you will be obliged to recognize that, even if you think me wrong, I am at least honest and consistent.' But history cannot prove the rightness of a cause. It is possible to be honest, and mistaken, to be right, and defeated. Accordingly Paul's second reaction is theology, on the basis of the Old Testament. I cannot forbear to point out in passing one inference that may be drawn from this. Paul believed that, in the stormy circumstances of the Church in his day, when the ship seemed in imminent danger of sinking, theology would prove both intelligible and relevant. It may be that if we prefer some other method, such as expediency and face-saving formulas, for the settling of church affairs, we are following the wrong line; equally, that if our theology proves irrelevant and unintelligible it may be less good theology than we thought it was. Paul at any rate thought theology a useful way of dealing with his church problems, and our immediate task is to examine the theology he uses.

The theology proper may be said to begin with 3.6. Before that come a couple of paragraphs in which history shades into theology. This is particularly true of the last paragraph of Galatians 2, which I left perhaps rather abruptly in my first chapter. The fact is that we are left in considerable doubt about what is happening at the end of chapter 2. Verses 11–14 are a reasonably clear description of circumstances and events in Antioch. Paul, as we saw, was ready to resist openly and violently the compromise course adopted by Peter and Barnabas at the bidding of James. The last sentence of verse 14 is undoubtedly as good a report of what Paul said to Peter as Paul's memory could supply. But where does Paul cease repeating what he said to Peter and begin to address the Galatians directly? Different answers have been given to this question, and I do not think it is worthwhile to pursue them here.[19] Paul himself might not have been very clear about the matter. He was reporting the Antioch incident because he believed it to be relevant to the situation in Galatia. He had no shorthand report or tape to check his memory. It seems clear that at 2.15 he is still speaking to Peter ('We are born Jews ...'), and there is no doubt whom he is addressing at 3.1 ('You foolish Galatians ...').

What is important to note at once, both for the present and as a pointer to what we shall encounter again and again in the epistle, is that Paul is arguing, and just beneath the surface of what he says you may easily find the thought, and often the language, of his opponents. It is there in 2.15: 'We are born Jews, and not sinners of Gentile stock' – sinners indeed, transgressors of God's law, by very reason of having been born Gentiles. This is the fundamental assertion of the Judaizing party who separate themselves from Gentile Christians and will not eat with them, the assertion that was taken up as axiomatic even by Peter and Barnabas. There is an absolute distinction, and it is the will of God that it should be so. It was God himself who, in the Old Testament, commanded his people to be separate from the rest of mankind (e.g. Isaiah 52.11), and from the time of Ezra Jews had been at pains to put this separation into effect. I emphasize this Old Testament background not to denigrate the Old Testament (there is much more to say about this) but to show that the attitude of the Judaizers was not unreasonable and not indefensible. It was not right, but in the form that James gave it, which did not deny the right of Gentiles to become Christians, it was not wicked, as it was with the false brothers who denied this right; and it was certainly not silly.

The trouble was that Peter, and the Jewish Christians who acted with him, were trying to combine this intelligible attitude with another, which is stated in verse 16, the attitude of the Christian who, by definition (and it is interesting that Paul can assume this definition) has become a Christian by believing in order to be justified. But why not, Peter might reply, justified by obedience to law? Here Paul replies with the trump card: Because Scripture itself declares this to be impossible! Paul quotes Psalm 143.2, 'By the works of the law shall no flesh be justified'. I say, 'quotes'; Peter might have replied (but Paul in the report if not in the event gives him no opportunity to do so), 'This is a misquotation'. So it is, at two points. One may be called a Freudian slip. Where Paul says 'no flesh' the psalm has 'no man living'. When he thinks of the unjustifiability of man before God he naturally speaks of man as *flesh*. I shall discuss Paul's use of this word later and therefore pass over it now. It is not important as a misquotation; the two expressions have essentially the same meaning; we may simply say 'No one' and leave it at that. More serious is the fact that Paul has introduced the words 'By works of the law', which are not in the text of the psalm. He might have defended himself by a two-pronged argument. In the first place, the psalm belongs within the context of Judaism and addresses Jews; if they are not to be justified they are clearly not being justified by works of law, which, *ex hypothesi*, they practise. In the second place, Paul can assume that if anything could justify man before God, obedience to the law that God himself has given would do it; since men are not justified, they are not justified in this way.

These two verses (15 and 16), taken together, explain the charge of hypocrisy that Paul brings against Peter and Barnabas in verse 13; at the same time they state the principle behind the rhetorical question of verse 14: 'How is it that you are compelling Gentiles to Judaize?' Peter is trying to combine two irreconcilable principles. The words quoted in verse 15 would not in themselves constitute hypocrisy; verse 16 is Paul's own understanding of the foundation of Christian life.

In verse 17 we can again hear an echo of the case that was brought against Paul in the argument, 'On your showing, Christ himself is a minister of sin', that is, he converts the law-observing Jew into a sinner. This is so appalling in both logic and theology that Paul can only say, 'God forbid!' It fails logically because Christ is not making anyone a sinner but revealing what the person already truly is, even though his sin is covered by a veil of legal piety. It fails theologically because it has not read to the end of the chapter; the goal of the process is righteousness. It is not Paul's theology but practical inconsistency that marks out the sinner. I cannot have it both ways; if I start to build up again the things which previously I pulled down I must have been wrong at some stage.[20] This is a proposition of general applicability, but it fits with the conversation with Peter (of which it may mark the end). Peter had begun to break down the middle wall of partition that separated Jew from Gentile; and now he is building it up again. If verses 15, 16 can mark what Paul means by hypocrisy in terms of theology, verses 17, 18 reveal it in practice; theology and practice are never far apart.

The next three verses present in concentrated form themes that will be more fully worked out in chapter 3, but we must look at them briefly now. The law played a real part in the business of salvation, but it was a limited part; its role came to an end in time. In chapter 3 this is set in a large context, the context of the working out of God's purpose in and for the world. This macrocosmic purpose and role are reproduced in the microcosm of the individual life; hence, 'through the law, I died to the law'. I died; that was the end of me in relation to the law and of the law in relation to me. It might have seemed better to say that the law died, and that this – a shocking paradox for a Jew – set me free to live to God. But this would not do (cf. Romans 7.1–6), for two reasons. One is that the law is not dead and done with; as a means of justification it is dead, but as a guide to the life of obedience it is not. The second reason is that Paul needs to speak not only of a death but of a resurrection also, and to do this means that he must speak of Christ and of human life in union with Christ. So – 'I died, crucified with Christ. Therefore I no longer live'. The old law–dominated, self-regarding life is gone. It is gone, however, to be replaced. 'Christ lives in me'. Some say that Paul is speaking here of baptism; it seems to me a striking fact that he does not mention baptism. He speaks of faith, for 'Christ lives in me' means substantially the same as 'I live by faith in Christ' (which follows). Faith (of which we shall hear more as we proceed) is a focusing of life on Christ, and a confessing of him; all this made possible by the primary fact of his love and self-giving.

The whole is summed up in verse 21. H. D. Betz (op. cit.,

p. 126) says that this refutes a charge. It may be so; but rather it is, or implies, a charge. Perhaps it flings back a charge in the teeth of those who made it. It is the Judaizers who nullify the grace of God; on their showing Christ might as well not have died. This for Paul is the ultimate *reductio ad absurdum*. It is not simply the sentimental reaction of one who happens to be attached to Christ as a person. That he should have died for nothing is in view of his resurrection unthinkable.

You may well think in these seven verses we have already had an adequate dose of theology. I could indeed have dealt with them at much greater length, and should have done so if they were not an anticipation of matters that we shall find discussed again, and perhaps made clearer because less epigrammatically, rhetorically, striking.

Before we move on to the material that will constitute the main substance of this chapter we have one more preliminary paragraph to look at. In 2.15–21, as I have said, Paul gives the substance of what he had said to Peter at Antioch, though as the passage continues, and especially in verses 19–21, he is, probably subconsciously, adapting it to the Galatian situation. With 3.1 he addresses the Galatians directly but in the light of what he has said at 2.21: 'If righteousness comes through the law, then Christ died for nothing.' The principle implied had been carried out in Galatia. Paul had laid the right foundation and the Galatians had begun in the right place. Christ crucified had been placarded before their eyes. But now someone had bewitched the poor fools, and Paul begins with a pragmatic argument cast in rhetorical questions. 'Consider the visible effects and accompaniments of the Christian life. You know that you received the Spirit; what was it that led to this? Did you perform actions in conformity with the law, and in return receive the Spirit? You know that you did not. What happened was that you heard the Good News and responded to it in faith; this was the sole and sufficient ground of the Christian experience you cannot deny that you had'. Paul repeats the question with more explicit reference to the outward, visible, phenomena that accompanied the preaching of the gospel and the gift of the Spirit. 'He who supplies the Spirit and does mighty works among you – does he do it because you kept the law or because you listened to the gospel with faith?' It is in a way a solid argument and it may have carried weight with some of the Galatians, but it is the sort of argument that can always be turned. Behind verse 3 we can detect (once more) the words of Paul's opponents. 'Yes, this was not a bad beginning for Gentiles. You began with faith, and God rewarded you beyond your deserts with spiritual gifts. Now in gratitude you must observe God's law, and in doing so you will ascend to new realms of the Spirit.' 'The reverse of the truth,' Paul replies; 'you began with the Spirit, which God gave you freely. To be circumcised now is to go back to the realm of the flesh.' Attempts to rise above the coarse earthy gospel by which God deals with men as they are finish by falling below it.

Thus Paul; but it must be admitted that at this stage of the argument it is, on the whole, his word against theirs. I shall come back (p. 46) to the question of the place that empirical argument may have in theology. Our next task must be to quarry the theological material contained in chapters 3 and 4. This is a considerable task.

I have already two or three times had occasion to point out that in Paul's words we can hear echoes of what his opponents were saying. He was arguing, and his arguments presuppose those against which he was contending, which we can therefore reconstruct. Now if it is true, as I believe it is, that there was a planned and concerted anti-Pauline movement which tracked the apostle through his various churches and put its alternative point of view, it should be possible to find out the beliefs of this movement and the arguments by which the beliefs were sustained. To Paul, these men were destroyers. They sought to substitute for the gospel he had preached, by which the churches had been founded, a different gospel which in fact was no gospel at all. Naturally the opponents saw this in a different light. It was not they who were false brothers, false apostles, but Paul. It was he who preached the wrong gospel, the wrong Christ, the wrong Spirit. His work must be counteracted and his disciples brought back from the error of their ways. As Jews, and one might add as Christians, they based their argument on Scripture, and the dispute is to a great extent one of exegesis. The inquiry into it will occupy most of this chapter. We shall gather things together in the third.

They began where Judaism began, with Abraham, and no doubt they quoted Genesis 15.6: 'Abraham believed God, and it was counted to him for righteousness'. It is clearer in Romans 4.1–3 than it is in Galatians that the text was used by Paul's adversaries, but having seen the fact in Romans we may understand it in Galatians 3.6, where the word ($\kappa\alpha\theta\dot{\omega}\varsigma$) which rather oddly introduces the new sentence and paragraph is probably to be taken in the sense: 'What I [Paul] have just said [in 3.1–5] is in fact not in disagreement but in accordance with Genesis 15.6'. That is, on Paul's interpretation of it. The Judaizers will have taken both 'believed' and 'reckoned' in a different sense. Abraham was an idolater who became a worshipper of the one God, and God rewarded him for this supremely good act, the desertion of heathenism and establishing of right belief, by taking this right belief as the righteousness that in fact it was. Abraham was the first monotheist, indeed the first Jew; and it was accordingly of prime importance to belong to the family of Abraham. It was to him and to his seed that God spoke the promises; outside this closed circle there were no divine promises, only threats. The normal way of entering the fortunate circle of the seed of Abraham was to be born into it by physical descent; this gave a firm (though not inalienable) title to the inheritance God planned for his people.[21] There was an alternative way in, by proselytization; for this circumcision was indispensably necessary. The uncircumcised receive short shrift in the Old Testament.

Another way of putting this was to say (as the Old Testament does) that God entered into covenant with Abraham. This was a covenant initially on a small scale, made between God and a family. Later it was expanded to cover the nation; this was the work of Moses. The new covenant was in several respects an advance on the old. The Abrahamic covenant was a simple compact between persons, though Abraham of course acted as the head of a family which, as the covenant itself declared, was to be extremely numerous. 'On that day the Lord made a covenant with Abram, saying, "To your descendants I give this land, from the river of Egypt to the great river, the river Euphrates"' (Genesis 15.18). A little later this covenant was given, on Abraham's side, one condition: 'This is my covenant, which you shall keep, between me and you and your descendants after you: Every male among you shall be circumcised' (17.10). The Mosaic covenant, however, was made between, on the one hand, God accompanied by the angels (ἐκ δεξιῶν αὐτοῦ ἄγγελοι μετ' αὐτοῦ, Deuteronomy 33.2),[22] and, on the other, Moses standing at the head of a numerous people. The Mosaic covenant, moreover, contained a large number of conditions: 'Behold the blood of the covenant which the Lord has made with you in accordance with all these words' (Exodus 24.8; for the 'words' cf. e.g. 20.1, 'God spoke all these words'). This abundance of legal conditions created a corresponding number of possible causes of disinheritance. The

Judaizers were able to draw attention to Deuteronomy 27.26: 'Cursed is everyone who does not abide in all the things that are written in the book of the law so as to do them'. The meaning (as evidently they argued) is plain: For salvation it is necessary to enter into the covenant made with Abraham, expanded, developed and enriched under Moses; and this means that the entrant must be circumcised and must thereafter keep the whole law.

This argument was reinforced by a homiletical interpretation of the story of Abraham, Sarah and Hagar, and their children, Isaac and Ishmael. It was undisputed, though perhaps embarrassing, that Abraham was not the father of the Jewish people alone. Before the birth of Isaac, Abraham, despairing of ever becoming a father, had begotten Ishmael by Hagar, a slave in his household. It was only later that, by divine intervention, he fathered Isaac by Sarah, a free woman and his wife. From this story it was inferred that the descendants of Isaac, Israel, were the true seed of Abraham over against the descendants of Ishmael. The significance of this was established by the quotation of Genesis 21.10, 12: 'Cast out the slavewoman and her son; for the son of the slavewoman shall not inherit with the son of the freewoman'. The moral was clear: There was no room in the people of God for any who were not sons of Isaac, that is to say, either born or adopted by the legal way into the elect family.

How does Paul deal with this argument? We start with the quotation in Galatians 3.6 of Genesis 15.6; as I have said, we are helped by the fact that the same passage is quoted in Romans 4.3. It is clear that between Galatians and Romans Paul has done a good deal of thinking and has strengthened his exegetical argument. In Romans he has two main points. Using the rabbinic exegetical device[23] known as *g^ezerah shawah* he allows the word 'reckon' to lead him from Genesis 15 to Psalm 32, and by combination of the two texts establishes the fact that the reckoning of righteousness is virtually equivalent to the non-reckoning of sin, and differs little from forgiveness. Certainly it is not a matter of totting up Abraham's good deeds and rewarding him accordingly. The second point Paul makes in Romans is the devastatingly simple observation that when God reckoned righteousness to Abraham, Abraham was still an uncircumcised, but believing, Gentile. Circumcision does not arise till Genesis 17. We must, I think, say that when he wrote Galatians Paul had not yet thought of either of these points. He remains closer to what is being argued by his opponents. As we have seen, they must have

24

claimed, 'It is all-important to be a child of Abraham'. With this claim Paul does not disagree; see 3.29, to which we shall come in due course; the end of his argument is, 'You are after all Abraham's seed'. The Judaizers, however, continued: There are two ways by which one may become a child of Abraham. The better is by birth; but for those who do not have that privilege there is always the possibility of circumcision later in life: become a proselyte by the approved means. Paul goes a different way. Children show their parents' characteristics; the essential characteristic of Abraham was (as Genesis 15.6 shows) faith; it follows that those who depend on faith, οἱ ἐκ πίστεως, are the sons of Abraham. The Judaizers have, as it were, given away their own case by admitting circumcised proselytes. If they had adhered to the principle of physical descent their definition of the sons of Abraham would have been watertight. But if others, not descended from him physically, are to be associated with Abraham, faith has at least as good a claim as circumcision to be the required qualification. Before leaving Abraham (for a moment) Paul produces another powerful (but not quite conclusive) argument. Scripture, that is, the Old Testament, itself shows that it was always God's intention that the Gentiles should join Abraham and his descendants as members of the people of God. At Genesis 18.18; 12.3 the Old Testament promises that in Abraham all the Gentiles would be blessed. Whether the LXX's ἐνευλογηθήσονται is a good rendering of the Hebrew *nibr^eku* may be questioned,[24] but the interpretation was not Paul's invention. To be a son of Abraham is to have a share in the blessing promised to Abraham; the blessing is to be accounted righteous, and others will receive this in the same way that Abraham did, by faith. So God justifies the Gentiles by faith (not by their obedience to law), and on the same basis they receive the blessing with Abraham – who is characterized not as circumcised (which he was not) nor as keeping the law before it was given (as some rabbis maintained) but as believing. Verses 6–9 form a rounded whole, pointing out the true significance of Abraham.

The Judaizers however still have up their sleeve the trump card of Deuteronomy 27.26, which I quoted above. The counterpart of blessing is curse; and Paul and his companions incur it. In the Old Testament, whose authority Paul cannot gainsay, it is written, 'Cursed is everyone who does not abide in all the things that are written in the law so as to do them'. This, surely, not only supports their own case but destroys Paul's, for notoriously he and his converts did not abide in all the precepts of the law. They did not accept the necessity of circumcision, they did not observe the food laws, and Paul speaks slightingly of the observance of festivals. Therefore he and his party are accursed. By an exegetical *tour de force* Paul not only rebuts but reverses this argument. It is not the Christians who know themselves to be free from the law who are accursed, but their opponents. This paradoxical conclusion is established in verses 11 and 12, and the argument is effective if its presuppositions are granted. The law has another word to say about the performance of commands: Leviticus 18.5, which declares, 'The man who has done them shall live by them'. But turning on to the prophets we have Habakkuk 2.4: 'He who is righteous by faith shall live' (it makes little difference if we order the words differently in English and read, 'He who is righteous shall live by faith'). Here is the man who will live; not the man who has achieved obedience to the law but the man whose trust in God constitutes righteousness for him. This (if related to Leviticus 18.5) must mean that men, even those who boast of the law and insist upon it, do not do what it commands; they do not abide in all the things that are written in the law; therefore even the Judaizers are under the curse of the law. The argument may appear tortuous to us, but it is not aimed directly at us. If the Judaizer appeals to Scripture to Scripture he must go; and Paul will beat him at his own game.

At his own game; but it would be wrong to suggest that Paul is here simply playing an exegetical game of words. There is serious theological matter under the surface. Before we attempt to dig it out, however, we must see what Paul makes of the fundamental issue of covenant. He starts from the convenient ambiguity of the Greek word διαθήκη. In common Greek usage it means a 'will' or 'testament', but in the LXX it appears as the equivalent of *b^erit*, usually translated 'covenant'. So the biblical word, the word used in the Greek Bible, turns out to have two meanings, and Paul is able to use both. Consider an ordinary testamentary disposition. When the testator has finished with it, no other person may alter it or add a codicil to it; this last word (ἐπιδιατάσσεται) is very important for Paul's argument. The διαθήκη is in final form, and no one may add to it. This is the initial premise. Paul adds a reminder, and a further note, which he will take up later. The reminder is that the Abrahamic covenant was based on promise – a free gracious promise, issuing from the primary freedom, God's freedom; no kind of trading was involved. The further note is that the promises were made to Abraham and to his seed (σπέρμα). Now both the English 'seed' and the Greek σπέρμα serve as collective nouns; that is, each implies, in ordinary use, a plurality. It would have been impossible to write in Greek καὶ τοῖς σπέρμασιν, as in English it would be impossible to write, 'And to your seeds'. But Paul notes the singular noun, and identifies the singular seed with Christ. He has often been blamed for this, and indeed it would be impossible for any of us to initiate an argument on these lines. But Paul is following his adversaries and must find means of countering their contention that only Jews, born and proselytized, might hope to enjoy the inheritance; and in doing so he finds a theological point of great importance, to which we shall come later. The fact that we should not choose to establish the point in this way does not undo its truth or diminish its importance. It is worthwhile to observe that the same understanding of the word 'seed' as capable of contraction to a single person occurs also in Romans 9, and that if it is correct (see above p. 25) to take descent to be marked out by characteristics, Jesus, rejected by Judaism and deserted by his disciples but acting in obedient trust in God, qualifies at the moment of crucifixion as the one seed.

The main point in Paul's present argument is that the law was given 430 years after the promise and therefore was in no position to change the terms of the διαθήκη. It cannot annul it; it cannot revoke the principle of promise, which must be regarded as fixed. One final stroke remains. The Judaizers could reply: 'But you forget. You say that no one can change the terms of a will; but there is one person who can do this, the testator himself. God is the testator, and God modified the original covenant-testament by giving the law'. 'No', Paul replies, 'the law was ordained by angels, by the hand of an intermediary. In contrast with the covenant of promise the law came only at second or third hand from God'.[25]

It remains only to consider how Paul deals with the argument based on Abraham, Sarah and Hagar.[26] He begins with the remark familiar to us in the form, 'Which things are an allegory,' ἅτινά ἐστιν ἀλληγορούμενα. Commentaries and dictionaries discuss the question whether this means, 'These things were written as an allegory', or 'These things are to be interpreted as allegories'. There is in the end little difference between the two; in either case we are transported into the Greek world of allegory. But Paul is arguing with Jews and we should begin in a different place. The adversaries have offered what would in Judaism be described as

$p^e\check{s}a\underline{t}$, 'interpretation' – a simple factual interpretation based on the literal meaning of the text. Paul, using a Greek expression that he never uses elsewhere, replies, 'This is the wrong way to interpret the text. It should be understood $k^emin\ homer$'. This is a recognized, non-literal way of dealing with a text, not exactly allegorical but near enough to this to warrant the use of the Greek word. The method involves (a) the reinterpretation of a significant word, and (b) the use of a parallel explanatory text. We shall see that Paul follows precisely these steps. First, he finds a means of identifying Hagar with Mount Sinai. How he does this is not clear. It may be that the suggestion, based on Arabic, to be found in the commentaries, is correct. Paul had spent three years in Arabia, and it would be surprising if he had not picked up some of the language. All that matters for the present is that he did make the identification (Galatians 4.25a). From it he deduces that Hagar stands for the covenant of the law; her children are the law-keeping Jews; she is a slave and so are her children. So the Jews and Judaizers, children of the Sinaitic legal covenant, are children of Hagar – slaves and (as regards the covenant of promise) illegitimate. So far Paul has made a negative point. Secondly, he moves across from the Genesis story to Isaiah 54.1 (quoted in 4.27: 'Rejoice, thou barren one'). The move is made on the basis of a common word. In the Genesis story Sarah is said to be 'barren', $^{\prime a}qarah$. Isaiah prophesies that, in the end, the barren woman will have more children than her rival. Whom does Sarah, barren but in the end bearing Isaac, represent? Jerusalem has been appropriated to Hagar, so that for Sarah Paul invokes the heavenly Jerusalem, a concept he does not develop.[27] This means that the future belongs not to law-keeping Jerusalem but to the company of justified sinners, who, whether Jews or Gentiles in origin, are children of promise, heirs of promise, in the same way as Sarah's son Isaac.

This brings us back to 3.29 and is the logical end of the argument, but Paul has two further points to make. The first confirms his conclusion. In the old story, particularly as expanded in traditional Jewish exegesis, Ishmael attacked Isaac. Here, says Paul, is a prophecy, and we are witnessing its fulfilment. Just as in the past he who was born according to the flesh, out of a purely human relationship, persecuted him who was born according to the Spirit, out of God's intervention, so now the Judaizers persecute us – and we may recall, for example, the perils from false brothers that Paul speaks of in 2 Corinthians 11.26. To make the second additional point Paul goes back once more to the Genesis story. The upshot of it all is, 'Cast out the slavewoman and her son, for the son of the slavewoman shall not inherit with the son of the freewoman' (4.30; Genesis 21.10). John Bligh[28] thinks that Paul was here calling for the expulsion of the Judaizers; I think he was doing something more terrible. He was stating the fact that by taking the line they had chosen they had excluded themselves not simply from the Church but from the eternal inheritance of the people of God.

There are a few points on which we should linger briefly here. First, Paul's argument is not empirical. He does not say, 'I have never met a man who kept the law properly'. Either instinct or prudence preserved him from this false step, for it is always open to the riposte, 'Ah, but I have – and you may next week'. Here, as in Romans 2, 3, Paul bases his indictment of human sinfulness not on observation (though on occasion he could use observation to illustrate the point, and with devastating effect) but on Scripture. Secondly, Paul's argument does not include such a heightening of the law as is found in for example the Sermon on the Mount, where it would be possible to imagine the debate, 'There are plenty of men who keep the commandment, Thou shalt not kill'. 'Ah, but did you ever meet one who was never angry?' 'There are plenty who abstain from adultery'. 'Ah, but did you ever meet one who never entertained a lustful thought?' Later in the epistle (5.14; see pp. 73, 74) we shall find Paul picking out the supreme commandment, the precept which no one fully keeps, but here his charge is not open to the countercharge that he has been tampering unfairly with the text of the law. Thirdly, Paul's argument does not excuse the Gentiles, even to the very limited extent to which Romans 2 may be said to do this. Romans 2 is indeed qualified by the string of Old Testament passages quoted in Romans 3.10–18, which was probably more effective than the somewhat involved logic of Galatians 3. But this argument has the effect of showing that all are under a curse, for it is clearly impossible to maintain that the Gentiles have observed everything written in the law. If Jews and Judaizers may be said to fall under the curse of Deuteronomy 27.26, so, *a fortiori*, do the Gentiles.

This observation leads Paul into what, from the point of view of the logical development of the argument, can be described only as a digression, but it is a digression full of the most important theological substance. We shall find that it is taken up later in the epistle, and it touches very closely on the theme of Freedom and

Obligation. I take it up here to bring the present chapter to its conclusion. All men, it seems, Jews and Gentiles alike, are under a curse which their disobedience to God has brought upon them. What can they do about this? The answer to this question is that there is nothing they can do; they cannot liberate themselves, and it is useless to speak of moral obligation to the unfree. The only thing that could be done God himself has done. This, as I say, is not strictly germane to the argument at the present point, and Paul, having left the thread of his argument at 3.13 will take it up again at 3.15. But he cannot pass by this vital point. Christ redeemed us from the curse of the law when on our behalf he himself became a curse. Here again Paul applies an Old Testament text which had probably been used against him, though not by the Judaizers, if they were in any sense recognizable as Christians. 'Cursed is everyone who hangs on a tree' (Deuteronomy 21.23). The Hebrew behind this is ambiguous; literally, 'A curse of God is everyone who hangs on a tree'. What kind of genitive is 'of God'? It seems that in the earliest period rabbinic interpretation took it as an objective genitive. The body hanging on a tree is an affront to God; it displeases him; it infringes his holiness. It was probably (we may guess) in the realm of anti-Christian propaganda that the genitive was taken to be subjective: 'God lays his curse upon everyone who hangs on a tree'. Paul may have used the text himself as he haled Christians off to prison. It must have seemed a most effective argument: his death on the cross proved that Jesus so far from being the Messiah stood under God's curse. That Paul remembered the Hebrew may be partly responsible for his saying that Christ became (not accursed but) a curse – an odd use of words. But subconscious recollection is not the whole point. It was impossible now for Paul the Christian to say that Christ was cursed by God; he was not. Paul (whether he remembered the Hebrew or not) chose to use the word expressing a relation. Christ came to stand in that position in relation to God that was rightly ours. There is a good parallel in 2 Corinthians 5.21, where Paul is careful not to say that God made Christ a sinner; he has already in the context defined Christ as the one who knew no sin. God did not make him a sinner; he made him to be sin – again the word of relation. Christ stood in that position in relation to God that is defined by the word sin. This (in 2 Corinthians) was in order that we might stand in that relation to God that is defined by the word righteousness; so here, Christ became a curse on our behalf that the blessing of Abraham might come to the Gentiles.

Paul is soon out of his digression; there will be more on these lines later, but we must not fail to observe that by this strange interchange between himself and us Christ redeemed (ἐξηγόρασεν) us. This is a fundamental verb of freedom. The slave is bought out of his slavery and becomes God's free man. Paul's theology is nothing if it is not a theology of freedom, though at present we hear little of what freedom is from and of what it is for, except in the reference to the Spirit,[29] received as at 3.2,5, by faith. There is much more on this theme to come.

THREE

The Theology of Freedom: The Decision

At the end of the last chapter we were obliged to stop part way through an account of Paul's theology as this is brought out in Galatians – a theology of freedom, expressed in recognized and enacted obligation. We followed Paul as he worked on the raw materials that he found in his environment, the primitive Christian tradition that he inherited and the arguments of his adversaries. The latter in particular we traced as they built up a theology which they could claim, with some show of reason, was founded on Scripture and described in accordance with revelation man's position in the presence of the gracious covenant-keeping God who expected in man a faithfulness matching his own.[30] God observed his side of the covenant, and man, provided by God with a wise law to guide him, must obediently observe his. This theological structure, still not without a specious attractiveness and reflected in some modern ways of understanding Christianity, Paul attacked at its roots, that is, in the exegesis on which it was founded. I shall not repeat his construction of an alternative exegesis; it was not an academic exercise but a fighting lawyer's speech, employing (as H. D. Betz has shown[31]) the methods and skills of the professional orator. I have given this third chapter the sub-heading 'Decision', for Paul's argument is designed, like all good speeches, and all good sermons, to win a verdict. The essence of it is summed up in paragraphs we have not yet studied; we must give them our attention now.

It is characteristic of Paul that from time to time he will stop in his tracks, wondering, it seems, if his argument has taken him too far, wondering, as many an orator has done, if his eloquence has led him to use words he might wish to reconsider. 'Do we then make void the law through faith? God forbid; on the contrary, we establish the law' (Romans 3.31). 'Shall we then continue in sin that grace may abound? God forbid' (Romans 6.1). This is a proper theological caution and we encounter it here in Galatians 3.19, 21. In the first place, if the law could not alter the basis of the covenant that God made with Abraham, why was it given at all? Was God wasting his own time and plaguing man unnecessarily? Paul has an answer to this question: which we shall consider in a moment, but it is one that seems to make the position even worse, and gives rise to a second question: Is the law contrary to God's promises? Have we now – inadvertently – proved that the law is a bad thing?

Why then the law? It may be that we hear again the voice of Paul's interlocutor: 'Your argument must be wrong because by leaving the law in a state of powerlessness in which it is unable to affect the relation between God and man you have robbed it of any reason for its existence. Yet God did give it, it is God's law, God's word, and therefore cannot be pointless and purposeless'. I am inclined however to think that for the present we have left the external questioner behind and are dealing with questions that arose in Paul's own mind. He had lived by the law; he still believed it to be a gift of God to man, the word of God, holy, righteous and good. He could not think it right simply to dismiss it. He knows that there is a gap in his argument that he must close, if only in order to satisfy himself. But his answer is a surprising one.

The law was added into the existing situation constituted by God's covenant with Abraham *on account of transgressions*. Traditional interpretation has taken this in the sense: 'in order to hold transgressions in check'. The law forbids man to do what is wrong and though it may not be completely successful it prevents the situation from getting out of hand. But this is not Paul's meaning. His meaning is given by Romans 5.20, which makes the same point in more explicit terms. The law crept in in order that transgression might abound – not to check it, then, but to multiply it. Whether the Galatians understood this truth, thus briefly, enigmatically expressed, I do not know. It would have helped them greatly if they could have read not only Romans 5.20 but the whole of Romans 5, especially 5.12–13. Sin has been in the world since the time of Adam; that is, it is coextensive with the human race and with all human history. But sin, ἁμαρτία, as Paul uses the word, is an abstract rather than a concrete term. It describes man as he declines from God, man centred upon himself, man falsely related to God. It is a pre-moral term, not yet denoting specific differentiated sins, such as murder, theft and adultery. In the absence of law there is no way of observing and assessing it; law was necessary therefore if man was to recognize himself as the sinner, the rebel against his Creator, that he undoubtedly was. Law was added to turn man's revolt against God into specific acts of transgression.

Paul adds (anticipating verses 23–5) that the law was given with a time limit. It was given 430 years after Abraham, so that it was not in at the beginning; and it would continue only till the seed should come which was envisaged in the initial promise to Abraham; that is, up to the time of Christ (3.16). The law had its part to play for a limited period, but it was never intended to be permanent. We shall take up this point later.

Well: the law is subsequent to the promise, 430 years later in Jewish history. It was not given in the same direct person-to-person way as the covenant of promise. It was not designed to be permanent. Its effect was not to create a sinless world but to make sin everywhere observable in the form of transgression. So should we draw the conclusion that the law is evil, opposed to God's gracious promises? No. Paul could give no other answer. It was unthinkable that God should simply contradict himself. The law had indeed but one fault, or rather defect. Its commands were good. Paul sums up the whole duty of man in a quotation from the Pentateuch (5.14; Leviticus 19.18). To be rightly related to God all that was necessary was that man should observe all the commandments of the law. Paul repeats this in Romans 2.13. The defect lay in the fact that man neither could nor even wished to observe all the commandments of the law. It was vain to quote (3.12), 'The man who has done them shall live by them', for man in his present state of death was unable to do them. It was like telling a starving man with an empty cupboard, All you need is a good meal. The law was not given to men living on good terms with God, living from God; in these circumstances (and it may have been so that Jews regarded the law) the law, duly observed, would have preserved them in life. It was given to men whose lives were already vitiated by sin, and in these circumstances it could only multiply transgression.

This is restated in the strongest terms in the next verse (22). 'Scripture' is probably a simple variant for law, though the article (ἡ γραφή) might suggest a particular passage. None however is quoted. Scripture has had the effect of locking up all things – the neuter expresses comprehensiveness and universality even more strongly than the masculine πάντας would do – under sin. It may in theory offer a way of life; in practice it signifies a sentence of death. There is no way to the presence of God by works of law, obedience and virtue; that way is bolted, barred and barricaded. But with the negative goes a positive proposition. Every other way of escape is blocked in order to make clear the one way that

God intends: 'that the promise might be given on the basis of faith in Jesus Christ to those who believe'. Note the repetition of the idea of faith, and the emphatic position of τοῖς πιστεύουσιν. It is the same way that Abraham followed, and there is no other (3.7, 9).

The next three verses (23–5) are remarkable for the string of temporal clauses they contain: 'Before faith came ... we were ... until faith should be revealed ... up to the time of Christ[32] ... but now faith has come ... no longer'. The temporary significance of the law is doubly underlined. That however is a proposition that must be carefully understood. It does not mean that there is ever a time when God ceases to be interested in the moral life of his children or to require their whole-hearted obedience. God acts, not along general lines of development, but at great moments in history: in covenant, with Abraham; by the law, with Moses; in fulfilment, with Christ. The law plays a significant part, but its role is done. It has served as gaoler, one might almost say, as Lord High Executioner (2.19); it was God's word, but God did not intend it to be his last word. I shall say more of this later; let us for the moment note the variety of language Paul uses to make his point. We are locked up under the guard of law; there is no escaping its verdict, so that there is no convenient non-moral by-path that might lead man to God – neither mysticism nor piety, neither cultus nor gnosis will enable man to escape. In verse 19 the limiting point was defined in terms of the seed of Abraham, Christ. Here the key word is faith: 'Before faith came ... till faith should be revealed ... that we might be justified by faith ... now faith has come'. Again we see the connection with Abraham; faith corresponds to the gracious promise, just as works correspond to law – at least to law as Judaism (according to Paul) had come to understand it. When every other possibility has been excluded, faith, and faith only, remains; and faith must be revealed (verse 23), it cannot be manufactured.

Paul exchanges the image of the prison for another, remembering perhaps (as in 4.1–4) that he is writing not to Jews but to Gentiles. Up to the time of Christ the law has been our παιδαγωγός – a word for which there is no single English equivalent. The older English versions have 'tutor' or 'schoolmaster', but the παιδαγωγός was not a schoolmaster, or a tutor (as that word is commonly understood). RSV has 'custodian', which suggests a caretaker; NEB's 'a kind of tutor' hands on the task to the reader; what kind? The παιδαγωγός did no teaching (so that we are not to think of the law as giving elementary religious instruction and then passing us on to Christ for higher studies); he was a slave, employed by a well-to-do master to accompany his son to school. He might carry the boy's books for him, but he was there to see that the boy did not run off and play truant. The picture changes but the thought is the same; no by-paths, the only way open is Christ. This emphatic Christocentrism is another way of saying faith. Christ has now come; so we have no more to do with the παιδαγωγός.

The equivalence of faith and Christ comes out in the opening sentence of the next paragraph, which marks the conclusion of the argument (3.26). Through faith, and in Christ, you are all sons of God. Faith has other consequences; rather, there are other ways of expressing the one consequence. Faith brings justification, that is, the rectification of man's relation with God. But who is rightly related to a father if his son is not? Paul in the context needs the concept of sonship not only because of its implication of intimate personal relationship but because he is using the concept of inheritance, and is moving from the notion of descent from Abraham to the even more fundamental notion of being children of God – and if children, then heirs (cf. Romans 8.17).

It is the 'in Christ' relationship, not sonship, that Paul is developing and illustrating when he goes on to refer to baptism. To be baptized is to come to be in Christ, just as dressing means getting into your clothes. Paul nowhere says that baptism is the only way into this 'being in Christ'; indeed, 1 Corinthians 1.14–17 suggests that he was somewhat indifferent about the matter. But it serves as a good image, possibly (though not certainly) because he has in mind that an adult convert being baptized, that is, immersed, in a river or lake, would first of all take off his clothes and then, after the baptism, put them on again. A putting off and a putting on were a visible part of the process, and the image of putting on Christ would suggest itself. Perhaps it was so. This was what happened to all who were baptized; they did not become sons of God independently of one another but jointly and corporately in Christ. The identification of Christ as the one seed of Abraham (3.16) is coming back into sight, though we have not yet quite reached it. In verse 28a Paul makes a further point. The essential thing, the thing that matters before God, is to be in Christ. The only distinction that concerns him is 'in Christ', 'not in Christ'. In this connection, but in this connection only, the difference between male and female ceases to exist.[33] Paul was not under the illusion that the coming of Christianity meant the obliteration of sexual differences. He knew that the male and female members of his churches would marry, and counselled them to marry. It would lead to problems, but to remain unmarried could lead to worse. And if they married, they should, he urged, marry properly, and not try to turn a physical relationship into a purely spiritual one. It should, Paul thought, be clear who was a man, and who a woman. He did not, for example, like unisex hairstyles; clearly because of his horror at the thought of any kind of homosexual relation. Men are and remain men, women are and remain women; but before God, in Christ, the distinction does not exist. Similarly with slaves and free men. Paul deals with the matter elsewhere in a practical way; the essence of his advice is that if, socially, you do not belong to the ranks of the free, you may as well put up with it; you have a better freedom than social freedom. But if a man is in Christ it makes no difference to God what his social status is. *In Christ*, there is neither slave nor free; the distinction is irrelevant. Christian freedom has many social implications, but it is theologically, not sociologically based.

In the same context we read, 'there can be neither Jew nor Greek', and draw the conclusion that, like sexual and social distinctions, racial distinctions are abolished in Christ. It is doubtful whether Paul was thinking of this. The Jews were not a popular people in the ancient world, but the attitude to them of Greeks and Romans was not based on racial considerations. 'I have called this antagonism racial for convenience. But this is misleading. Though Greeks and Latins refer to the Jews as an ἔθνος or a *natio* or a *gens*, i.e. a folk or tribe, there is no genuinely racial or racist connotation. The distinction is political, social and religious, national rather than genetic. The large mass of converts among other peoples prevented the racial idea from developing. Besides, the Jews of Judaea would not differ physically from other Aramaic or Greek-speaking inhabitants of the Levant.'[34] The distinction, or non-distinction, between Jew and Greek is the same here as elsewhere in the Pauline letters. It is the distinction between the religious and the irreligious, between the covenanted and the uncovenanted, that is abolished in Christ. Abraham is the ancestor of all believers, of the Jew who sees through the precepts of Torah to its real requirement of faith rather than works, and sees that faith directed towards Christ, and of the Gentile who has the work of the law written in his heart and trusts Christ, knowing that he has no religious works to offer. Of course it is also true, and a necessary consequence of Paul's words, that as differences between the sexes remain in fact, so differences between races persist, but all these differences become, in the area denoted by 'in Christ', not merely irrelevant but non-existent; God pays no heed to them, and men should follow his example. Racial harmony must follow from what Paul says, but he is working at a deeper, more fundamental level than the sociological. You may have behind you an ancestry that reaches back through Moses to Abraham, or you may not; no matter. What does matter is that you be in Christ.

All this is negatively put. Its positive counterpart is that you are all one person in Christ Jesus. I do not think that Paul is here working in terms of the concept of the body of Christ, which he uses elsewhere. The noun we must put with the numeral 'one' is 'son'.[35] Paul remembers, and is now about to return to, his (to our minds) forced observation regarding the 'one seed' of Abraham (p. 27). *You* are the one seed; Paul declares this explicitly in 3.29. If you belong to Christ (a variant way of saying 'If you are in Christ'), then you are Abraham's seed (σπέρμα, singular), heirs (κληρονομοι, plural) in terms of promise. Of course Paul knows that 'seed' is a collective noun, but it was necessary for him first to break down the old collectivity of race in order to establish the new collectivity which is coming into being, in an inconceivable unity, with and in Christ. The curious verbal trick proves to be the key to the whole argument. God's age-old purpose of blessing, clarified and sharpened by the antithetical action of the law, is now realized in Jesus and in those who are in him.

So much for this great chapter. I hope a coherent line of argument has emerged; if it has not, the fault is mine. But we have more to do before we stop and try to see as a whole the theology Paul has been developing. So far he has presented a closely reasoned case based upon a controversial exegetical discussion of the Old Testament texts which both he and his opponents recognized as authoritative. Perhaps it occurred to him – it should have occurred to him – that his readers in the Galatian churches were less familiar with the Old Testament than he was. Abraham, Moses, covenant, law – these were part of a technical language in which he had been educated and they had not. He must restate his argument for the benefit of the Galatians, who, however attracted to Judaism they may have been, were Gentiles and at home in the Gentile world. But of course they knew about heirs and the inheritance an heir might hope eventually to receive. What of the case where the heir is a minor? The situation is not uncommon and most reasonably developed legal systems make provision for it.

Paul can assume that the Galatians will understand. The infant heir, though potentially the master of the whole estate, is during his legal infancy no different from a slave. This is a familiar legal situa. tion, and Paul immediately begins to apply it. We too have known what it is to be in the position of slaves. This reminds the reader of the state of man under the law of Moses, but here there is no reference to the law. We were enslaved under the elements of the cosmos. Paul has abandoned the language of Judaism for that of astrology and gnosticism, believing, no doubt correctly, that this will be familiar to his readers. The elements are the cosmic powers; perhaps spiritual beings inhabiting the skies, perhaps the stars themselves personified. It is worthwhile to look for a moment at the world-view behind the terminology. Men lived on a flat earth, above which stretched a number – probably seven – of concentric hemispherical shells. In these moved the seven planets. Above was the world of spirit, incorruption, immortality – of God. Below lived men, material, corruptible, mortal. The regularity of the planetary motions had long been observed, so majestic and orderly that it was understood as a symbol if not the actual mechanism by which destiny reigned in the affairs of men. Man's only hope was to escape through the hemispheres and so find his way into the upper world of light and life. Astrology was content to wait for a message from the stars; gnosticism offered the vital knowledge of self, the universe and its lords that would provide the password of escape; sacramental rites were called in to aid man's deliverance. But it was common ground that man, unless he received some special aid, was enslaved under the cosmic elements which rule by destiny. Paul saw no reason to contradict this view. Mankind was enslaved – until the moment came for God to act. This moment is defined without any explicit reference to the fulfilment of prophecy. When the time was ripe God acted, sending forth his Son. Is this a further piece of gnosticism? the myth of the descending redeemer? This is too large a question to discuss here, but it seems probable that Paul was making a contribution to what was later to be a full-blown myth rather than taking one over (cf. Philippians 2).[36]

Paul's redeemer is a man: born of a woman. There is no hint of the virgin birth here. Those born of women are human beings, as at Matthew 11.11. Jesus Christ may be more than man, but he shares both the resources and the limitations of human existence.

There is however another aspect of real humanity, expressed in the next words: 'born under the law', born that is under God's command, under obligation to do God's will. Part of Paul's meaning is that Jesus was a Jew, but only part; Jesus was part of creation, owing obedience to the Creator. This is something that Paul is unable to describe without the use of the word law, and though he is careful not to define law in explicitly Mosaic terms, and some could have read the passage and seen in it no more than a reference to the law of the planets, when read in its context it cannot fail to recall the discussion of law in chapter 3.[37] To be under the law is to be enslaved; man is not free, and his position calls for redemption, the process by which slaves are liberated. The word (ἐξαγοράζειν) is the one that was used at 3.13. Law here means slavery, as there it meant curse. The law lacks only the power to give life (3.21), but lacking this it can only enslave and curse. Again – and I must underline the point – Paul's theology appears as a theology of freedom; its very heart is the act by which God through his Son sets men free. But verse 5 contains a second purpose clause.[38] The same act that leads to redemption from servitude leads not to complete independence but to υἱοθεσία, adoption; not detachment from the *pater familias* but a new relationship with him. Before his conversion, said John Wesley, he served God as a servant; afterwards he served him as a son.

The paragraph ends with a return to the themes of 3.1–5. Paul takes up again his reference to the Spirit, this time with an objective emphasis, which balances the subjective in chapter 3. You were not made sons of God by the ecstatic phenomena of the Spirit. Because you were already, objectively, related to God as his sons, made such by faith and in Christ, God sent forth his Spirit. It is the same verb (ἐξαπέστειλεν) that Paul used of the Son in 4.4. In a comparable mission the Holy Spirit came into our hearts, crying out Abba, Father. This is not the place to discuss the Aramaic background of this word, so surprisingly introduced into a Greek text.[39] It is enough to say that it was characteristic of Jesus and thus has the effect of aligning our sonship with his. Because you are sons God sent the Spirit of his Son into your hearts, so that you address him in the same terms as your elder Brother. It is the 'in Christ' again. *In Christ* we are righteous, *in Christ* we are sons.

The question is raised here, as it was in 3.1–5; What does Paul understand by the gift of the Spirit? Does the crying of the Spirit represent some kind of inspiration? Does the use of the non-Greek word suggest the practice of glossolalia, and that this phenomenon was the utterance not of unintelligible sounds (1 Corinthians 14.6–12) but of foreign languages not known to the speaker's intellect (Acts 2.8, 11)? Or have we to do not with inspired speech but with something no more abnormal than the sincere and convinced repeating of the *Pater Noster*? It would be unwise to give a different answer here from that which was given in respect of 3.1–5. There it seemed unlikely that the work of the Spirit was thought of as a matter of inspired speech; it was rather to be seen in the existence of a Christian community, living by faith and united about the person of Jesus. Similarly here, Paul is thinking of a fundamental feature of Christian existence, the freedom of approach to the Father that every Christian has. It may but need not be expressed in excited speech.

The conclusion follows at once. You, the believer, are not a slave, but free. You are a son, and therefore an heir of God. The non-Jewish form of the argument has led to the same conclusion as 3.29. And here the epistle might happily end. The Gentiles have been gathered into the people of God.

The letter does not end here because of the catastrophe in Galatia which evoked it. Gentiles already Christian are being urged to become Jews. Why not? They were throwing away the freedom Christ had given them.

Paul first goes back to the Galatian past which he had already described in 4.3 (p. 39). They were enslaved to the cosmic elements, here described as beings which essentially were not gods. Paul does not say what they were; he does not say that they did not exist. Whatever they may have been they were not what he, Paul, meant by God – the God of the Old Testament, the God and Father of Jesus Christ, the only God there is. Was this enslavement an objective or a subjective bondage? Did the heavenly powers exercise through destiny a real constraint upon those whom they were able to get in their grip? Or did the bondage exist – really exist – only in the minds of those who experienced it, whose belief in the force of destiny left them unable to control their own fate? The present small paragraph hardly gives us evidence enough to decide this question, but we must bear in mind that objective and subjective elements run side by side throughout both Paul's account of man's plight and his account of salvation; also that what I have described as subjective bondage is in its own way at the same time objective. A man hypnotically convinced that his hands are bound cannot move them. We shall return to this question (pp. 88f.).

Liberation from bondage is described, in the first instance, in terms so thoroughly gnostic that it is hard to suppose that they did

41

not come from pre-Christian gnostic theology.[40] The time of bondage corresponded with the time of ignorance of God; coming to know God meant release from bondage. I doubt whether Paul would have expressed himself as he does if he had not been familiar, and expected the Galatians to be familiar, with this kind of proposition, since he goes on immediately, not to reject it altogether (since it contains an element of truth) but to qualify it. Knowing God is very well, but the primary and essential thing is being known by God, who might be expected to refuse to recognize his disobedient and unworthy creatures. It is worthwhile to linger for a moment over this point since it is (as far as Galatians is concerned) a new way of expressing a truth Paul has other ways of stating – the truth that it is always God who takes the initiative in relations between himself and man. Obedience to the will of God expressed in Torah is (like knowledge of God) good, provided that it is remembered that God's grace, not man's work, takes priority. Righteousness must be served (Romans 6.18) but righteousness begins as God's gift of a proper relation with himself. The fundamental truth expressed in the doctrine of justification occurs in passages where the word is not found.

Knowing God, known by God, the Galatians have escaped from servitude to the cosmic elements. Is it conceivable that they should now propose to return to this state from which they have recently emerged? This rhetorical question, and the positive implication that lies behind it, are one of the most remarkable statements in the whole of the Pauline corpus. The Galatians, he implies, are going back to their old pagan life under the rule of destiny and the stars. But they were not returning to pagan life; they were, some of them, submitting to the argument that they should accept circumcision and other regulations of the Jewish Torah. This, according to Paul, was a return to paganism – an extraordinary proposition to come from a Jew who in earlier days had surpassed all his contemporaries in enthusiasm for the ancestral religion. It is not hard to see pointers to what was in his mind. We recall Paul's acceptance of the Jewish tradition that on Mount Sinai the law was delivered to Moses by angels, and it was easy to identify angels with the heavenly beings who ruled the skies and what happened beneath them. When Paul goes on to illustrate what the Galatians were doing he specifies their observance of days, months, seasons and years; and of course the calendar was controlled by the movements of the celestial bodies. These however are only hints. The main point is that by allowing themselves to be absorbed in the practices of religion, of any religion, the Galatians were turning to something that is less than God, to things, beings, which in their very essence are not God. And if this were to happen (Paul will not allow himself to believe that it really has happened) all his work would have been lost, for his apostolic message consisted in the summons to turn away from all human achievements to the one place where the true God in his mystery and power was to be seen, in the placarding of Christ crucified.

We have now surveyed the theological substance of the chapters that form the theological core of the epistle.[41] In the next paragraph (4.12–20) Paul switches back to autobiography and his past relations with the Galatian churches. He would probably have denied that there was any real change of subject matter, for he saw his life as determined by theological considerations: 'I do all things for the sake of the Gospel' (1 Corinthians 9.23). But his present hurt was personal and not merely intellectual. I have looked briefly at this paragraph in the first chapter, and shall now mention outstanding points as briefly as may be. (1) There was a time when everything went well (4.13–15).[42] (2) Such friendship as was then established should be able to stand up to the strain of speaking the truth (4.16). (3) Deterioration in their relations had been caused not by Paul's plainness of speech but by others who had come to Galatia and were paying court to the Galatians, trying to get hold of them (ζηλοῦσιν, 4.17, 18). (4) Paul claims no exclusive rights over the Galatians; let others come and win their love so long as they do not pervert the gospel and ruin Paul's work (4.18). (5) In a striking but somewhat mixed metaphor Paul describes the sorrow he feels as birth pangs; he is in travail with the Galatians, not that they may be born again (an image that Paul does not use) but that Christ may be formed in them (4.19). The new metaphor takes up the substance of 4.6; what Paul seeks is the reproduction of Christ's sonship in those to whom he writes. (6) But, in the end, what can he, what can anyone do by letter? He cannot see how they are responding to what they read. If he could see the beginning of penitence, a longing for a return to the good days of the past, reflected in their faces, he could change his tone, give up the language of angry rebuke, and comfort them. As it is, he must go on taking the risk of telling them the truth (4.20).

The truth is theological truth. Paul cannot write impersonally, but he is not asking for personal favours. The question is not whether the Galatians like him better than the Judaizers, but whether his theology or theirs is true. The two theologies confront each other. We must conclude this chapter by looking at them both.

What was the theology of the Judaizers? In the second chapter we saw enough of their arguments to reconstruct it to some extent. We can see the Old Testament passages they drew upon and the kind of exegesis they used. Paul was obliged to follow them from point to point because he could not afford to let it appear that his opponents had the Old Testament – the Bible – on their side. I see no reason to doubt that Paul was giving an honest picture of those with whom he was dealing. But they were bitter enemies whom he was prepared to anathematize because they were destroying his churches and leading his people into what he conceived to be damning error (5.2, 4). Is his account fair? Is it accurate? It seems to me to tally in some remarkable ways (though not in every way) with the covenantal nomism of E. P. Sanders.[43] The covenant begins with Abraham, and the crucial question is why it begins at all. Does it begin with a command – 'Go from your country and your kindred and your father's house to the land that I will show you' (Genesis 12.1) – a command which Abraham religiously, virtuously and obediently accepts, thereby deserving the accreditation of 'righteous' and partnership in the covenant? Or does it begin with a pure act of grace in which God freely chose a Mesopotamian idolater and accounted him righteous on the basis of nothing but his obedient trust? We have no means of answering this question except the fact that Paul could hardly have written as he did had he supposed that the Judaizers accepted what he understood as the principle of grace. At all events the call and the promise came to be combined with the notion of law, of commandments which must be kept if the well-being of the people and of the individual within the people was to be assured. This means that, whether or not we speak of covenantal nomism, whether or not we understand the promise to precede the law, law has taken over, and obedience to law becomes the touchstone of salvation. And though the student of Judaism has long since grasped the fact that the law was regarded as a delight and a privilege, a gracious gift of the good God (which is how Paul himself conceived it), he does no injustice to Judaism – certainly none to the Judaizers as described by Paul – if he bluntly states their fundamental principle as: If you observed the law you were in, and if you failed to observe it you were out.

Did freedom and obligation have any meaning to the Judaizers?

To answer 'No' would do them an injustice, notwithstanding their intention of 'bringing us into bondage' (2.4). It was a fundamental proposition, which they must have shared, that the law made man free so long as he continued in obedience to it. An interesting piece of haggadic interpretation is given in Mishnah Aboth (6.2). It begins with the negative statement:

> Every day a *bath qol* goes forth from Mount Horeb, proclaiming and saying, Woe to mankind for their contempt of Torah, for whoever does not occupy himself in the study of Torah is placed under a ban (*nazuph*), as it is said (Proverbs 11.22), As a golden ring in the snout (*nezem zahab b$^{e'}$ap̄*) of a swine, so is a fair woman without discretion. And it is said (Exodus 32.16), And the tables were the work of God ... graven, (*ḥaruṯ*) upon the tables. Read not *ḥaruṯ* but *ḥeruṯ*, freedom, for you will find no free man but him who occupies himself with Torah. But everyone who occupies himself with the study of Torah, he shall be exalted, as it is said (Numbers 21.19), From Mattanah ('a gift') to Nahaliel ('God has led me'), and from Nahaliel to Bamoth ('high places').

One's first impulse is to dismiss this passage as too late to have any relevance to a study of first-century Judaizers. The Mishnah, based for the most part on older materials, was compiled about AD 200, but the tractate Aboth in its original form had only five chapters. The sixth, from which our quotation is taken, was added at a considerably later date. But the sayings are ascribed to Joshua b. Levi, of the middle of the third century, and the same exegesis in the same form (known as *'al-tiqre'*: read not...but...) is attributed in Erubin 54a to another rabbi, Aha b. Jacob (*c.* AD 330): 'If the tables had not been broken no nation or tongue would have had power over the Israelites, for it is written' (and here Exodus 32.16 follows, as in Aboth 6.2). The same word (to occupy oneself, *'-s-q*, in various forms) is used by R. Meir (*c.* AD 150) in Aboth 4.10: 'Engage not over much in business (*'eseq*) but occupy thyself (*^{a}soq*) with Torah; and be lowly in spirit before all men. If thou neglectest the law many things neglected shall rise against thee; but if thou labourest (*'amalta*) in Torah he has abundant regard to give thee.'

Of the saying of Joshua b. Levi, David Daube[44] says that it 'may be directed against, and therefore dependent on, the Christian view of freedom, which implied an abandonment – a partial one at least – of the Law. But' (Daube adds) 'the principal insight inspiring the saying can be shown to be extremely ancient.' It is tempting to say that we have in '-s-q, 'occupying oneself' (with Torah), the linguistic background of Paul's ἔργα νόμου 'works of law', but that, I suspect, makes things too easy. We shall come later to a consideration of what Paul has to say about the law. For the Judaizers, it seems, freedom comes through the due discharge of obligation.

What of Paul's theology? It ought to be said at the outset that though Paul may have had a systematic theology he did not see fit to write it out in his letters, not even in Romans, certainly not in Galatians. It would be hard to imagine anything less coolly systematic, though it is coherent, organic and very powerful. That is why I have allowed Paul first to speak as he himself chooses before, at the end of our work on the theology of the letter, we attempt to sum up the contents and characteristics of his theology. At this point, therefore, the following account is no more than a sketch.

One question that arises is the place of empiricism in theology, the appeal to experience. Is this valid? If so, within what limits? When Paul moves on from his recollection of the affair at Antioch he begins with the question, 'This is all I want to learn from you' (3.2), as if nothing else mattered. It is surely clear that the method is not invalid; if it were, Paul would not use it. Yet it is equally clear that it is not in Paul's opinion adequate, or he would not go on to take further steps; at least, the arguments of his opponents must be answered with arguments. He appeals to the gift of the Spirit and the working of miracles; we saw earlier that what is behind this is the existence of a Christian community, which came into being not through the promulgation of a law, met by obedience, but by the preaching of a gospel, met by faith. The whole process which led to the existence of Galatian Christianity began in this way. This means that there is little to be found here of the objectification of religious and moral values (to which I shall return shortly under another heading). Paul's criteria are neither doctrinal nor institutional, but the transformation of life in love. Even so, however, his position is a difficult one, for there may be little observable difference between the fruit of the Spirit and works of law. He is obliged to walk on a knife edge between the alternatives of flinging away the moral content of Christianity and the conversion of it into a new legal system. Without the theological argument that follows, 3.1–5 might be impossible to maintain. In the history of Christian thought there have been too many attempts to have experience without theology, and theology without experience.

In chapter 3 Paul touches several times on the theme of righteousness and justification. There are other important passages in chapters 2 and 5. There is of course even more material in Romans, and the subject could form the theme of a whole course of lectures; a paragraph must seem inadequate especially in view of important recent discussions of the questions involved. Thus for example Ernst Käsemann and Peter Stuhlmacher[45] have argued that the righteousness of God is essentially his faithfulness to that relation with men that he established by creating them. Because he is their Creator he is under obligation to perfect his creation, bringing it back into relation with himself when it strays from him. Others again, from Albert Schweitzer onwards,[46] have argued that other themes, the mysticism of being in Christ, the relation of Jew and Gentile within the people of God, are more central and seminal in Paul's theology. Clearly we cannot here discuss these matters at length, but we may bear them in mind as we concentrate our gaze on Galatians.

Attention is rightly drawn to a number of Old Testament passages where God's righteousness seems to be virtually equivalent to salvation. The two terms appear in synonymous parallelism. 'My righteousness is near, my salvation is gone forth' (Isaiah 51.5); 'The Lord hath made known his salvation: his righteousness hath he openly shewed in the sight of the nations' (Psalm 98.2). The link between the two concepts is significant, but it is important to see where it comes from. In the Old Testament God's saving righteousness is always for those who are (at least) relatively righteous. He sees that they get their deserts. Thus he brings his people to exile in Babylon in righteous punishment; they get their deserts, for they have been disobedient and rebellious; then they got double their deserts (Isaiah 40.2). And now the Jews are better than the Babylonians who oppress them, so that the manifestation of God's righteousness, his fair, judicial action, will mean that the Jews are set free, and incidentally that the Babylonians get their share of punishment: no salvation for them, though they too are God's creatures. This is not the situation Paul is dealing with. Scripture, he says, has shut up the whole universe under sin (3.22). 'There is none righteous, not so much as one' (Romans 3.10). Yet God's judgement issues nonetheless, for those who have faith, in the verdict of acquittal; not through negligence, not through a legal fiction, but through a creative act in grace, in which God rectifies man's relation with himself. There is in fact no serious understanding of righteousness and justification except in the context of the courtroom; yet this is like no other courtroom, in that the judge takes the prisoner's part and reconciles him to himself. This is the divine initiative that is the core of Paul's gospel; it was interesting to observe it earlier (p. 42) in relation to a different set of concepts (knowledge). The core of Paul's gospel; also the core of the story of Jesus, who as the friend of tax-collectors and sinners brought the prodigals back to God. There is a question here over which we may pause for a moment. Most of us would, I think, find it natural to do what I have just done; that is, to move back from Paul's technical forensic language to the story of Jesus, where we see justification in personal action. Paul does not do this; instead he goes back to the, to us, somewhat obscure Old Testament story of Abraham. Why? There is no single answer to this question. For one thing, Paul may have been less familiar than we are with stories from the life of Jesus – there are notoriously few in the epistles. Again, his opponents probably appealed to the story of Abraham, so that Paul was obliged to deal with it for controversial reasons. He must show that the father of the race was on his side. Moreover, they probably, in dealing with Abraham, stated the question in the form, 'How does one become a member of the people of God, a member of the Abrahamic family which stood in a covenant relation with God?' Finally, it was important to Paul as a theologian to show that what God did in Christ was not a mere happy afterthought, as if God had said first, Let's try the law as a means of keeping the human race right, and only when that failed found that he had better think again and try the gospel instead. In fact, God had in mind one continuous saving operation. From the beginning, from the time of Abraham, the whole process was in his mind.

This leads to a third theme. I spoke of one continuous operation. This would be very well if we proceeded straight from Abraham to Christ, but what of the law? Does this not break the continuity? I have already hinted at an answer to this question, but I must develop it now. Law as it exists in Judaism, and as Paul views it, is the objectification of religion and morality. Man is a religious and moral creature; the religion may be bad religion, or instinctive religion, the morality unthinking and corrupt, but both exist. Torah objectifies them in concrete form. Religion is to be not merely a feeling of awe in the presence of the transcendent, but the performance of specific cultic acts, such as sacrifice, or circumcision; morals are not identified with custom, the instinct of the herd, or with a universal categorical imperative, but obedience to such commandments as 'Thou shalt not kill, Thou shalt not steal, Thou shalt not commit adultery'. Now this objectification of religion and morality is a dangerous business, and this is nowhere made clearer than in the New Testament. Man seizes upon the precept that he shall, for example, circumcise his children, and supposes that by obeying this precept he has given God his due and need have no personal dealings with him in faith and love. He seizes upon the prohibition of murder and observes it, thinking that he has thereby satisfied God's ethical requirements. What this means is that he has climbed up the signpost and perched himself on top of it, instead of following the road the signpost pointed out to him; and this is not the way to use a signpost, even when the signpost is provided not by moral philosophy but by the providence of God. For the divine law is God's own crystallization of religion and morality, the crystallization of something otherwise diffused in history and in the universe. The days, months, seasons and years of 4.10 are significant; the law is tied up with them, with the structure and motion of the universe itself; and such ethical precepts as 'Thou shalt not kill' are not peculiar to the Bible. The danger of objectifications and codifications of religion and morality has been clearly perceived in our time; hence the revolt against religion and moral law, the quest for 'religionless Christianity', and situation ethics. But these movements have missed the real drive of the Pauline criticism, which aims not to abolish the religious and moral laws but to live in constant tension with them. Paul's teaching about the law has two elements. On the one hand, the law is the enemy, in some ways the supreme enemy of mankind, and as such it is overthrown by the gospel. On the other hand, the law is the word and will of God, holy, righteous, good and spiritual; therefore never to be despised. The tension between these two attitudes corresponds to the tension of apostolic Christianity; more of this in the next two chapters, in which I shall develop the theme. For the present, note the understanding of history that is involved. The law of Moses was not (for Paul) an unfortunate slip on God's part which spoiled the otherwise smooth progression from Abraham to Christ, nor was it a change in the basic character of the covenant. God so established the pattern of morals and religion as to make it impossible for man simply to play at cultus or to play at ethics. He demanded that each should be taken so seriously that men should be compelled to recognize that neither could ever provide a satisfactory basis for their relation with their Creator. Just as the positive relation of Abraham to God pointed to the fulfilment of the promise in Jesus, so the negative relation of Moses to God pointed to the fulfilment of the law in Jesus. The righteousness of God manifest in Christ is attested by the law and the prophets.

Finally we must consider the characteristics of the theology Paul is forging on the Galatian anvil. It is a controversial theology. This is clear to the most superficial reader and it has been demonstrated in a particularly convincing way by H. D. Betz's rhetorical analysis of the epistle.[47] It may be that Paul conformed a little less closely than Dr Betz suggests to the contemporary models of courtroom and similar speeches, but taken on the whole the parallels are convincing. It might seem at first sight that though this might make Galatians interesting from the point of view of ancient history and literature it would reduce its practical significance for our own time. Its theology was adapted to the controversy that had erupted in Galatia and is therefore (one might argue) not adapted to ours. It is true that there are places where Paul expresses himself in a way that would be for us unnatural, perhaps impossible; but it would be unwise to infer that the theology itself (as distinct from the mode of expression) was inappropriate to the changed circumstances of the twentieth-century church. It was controversy that made Paul's theology what it was (as it was controversy that made Luther's – in each case it is possible to watch the man's theology grow as he had new issues to face and fight), and Galatians is at the heart of the most fundamental of all controversies, the controversy that threatened to turn the gospel into something that was not a gospel. The theology that was hammered out in controversy was welded into a whole, and the theology of Galatians is at the heart of the whole Pauline system. It is not itself the whole: anything less like a *Summa Theologica* it would be hard to imagine. But it is one of the creative springs of the whole, and if Paul's theology has any permanent value this can be perhaps best exercised through Galatians, provided that the reader is prepared to be patient with the language and penetrate beneath its surface to its meaning.

A controversial theology: it is perhaps only to define this description more precisely if we add, a critical theology. Neither Paul nor his opponents felt obliged to abstain from personalities, but Paul himself worked primarily in the field of ideas, addressing searching questions to the theological environment in which he found himself. If we may accept his own description of himself (Galatians 1.14), he had been excessively zealous for the ancestral traditions of his people. His conversion changed that; his discovery that Jesus was alive made him question and rethink both the eschatology and the legal systems in which he had been brought up.[48] Jesus, raised by God from the dead, could hardly be less than the Messiah; the Messiah had therefore already come; what did it mean to live in the messianic age? In what sense had he and others been delivered from the present evil age (1.4)? Again, the legal system as currently administered had condemned Jesus, who had now been proved to be in the right; if he had not been, God would not have raised him from the dead. So had Paul and his fellow experts misunderstood the Torah of the Old Testament? Was Torah itself not the way to God that Judaism had taken it to be? It was not only Judaism that was subject to this critical inquiry. I have said in the first chapter that already as a persecutor Paul must have been aware of what Christians believed was true. This did not mean, however, that Paul was content simply to go on repeating what had already been said by those who were apostles before him (1.17). It is possible (less frequently in Galatians than in other epistles) to see him questioning traditional formulas. This was partly in a controversial sense, as in the exegetical debates of Galatians 3. But the questioning process was not only controversial. Paul asked questions because they occurred to him as they did not always occur to others, and he wanted to know the answers. Thus in 1.4 (cf. 2.20) he says that Christ gave himself for our sins. We know that this was a traditional, pre-Pauline, Christian belief because Paul quotes similar words at 1 Corinthians 15.3, introducing them with the words, 'I handed on to you that which also I received.' It is easy (and for the majority quite satisfactory) to be content with such a proposition. Paul is not. He develops it in terms of justification (which is not only an anti-Judaizing device), of sacrifice, of a parallel with Adam, of the curse of hanging, and so on.

It is possible to see here already the twin themes of freedom and obligation in relation to theology, that is, to the work of the theologian. Paul refuses to be bound by conventional formulas (which we now can see to have been more common in his time than was formerly supposed). If they are satisfactory he will quote them, but he is free to modify and expand them. Notwithstanding the converting revelation of Jesus Christ he (eventually) visits Peter and James in Jerusalem (1.18f.), ready to make contact with

Peter and James in Jerusalem (1.18f.), ready to make contact with them and learn what they have to say (ἱστορῆσαι); but he is not unduly impressed by them. 'Whatever they were makes no difference to me' (2.6). 'He who is troubling you shall bear his burden, whoever he may be' (5.10; was this James?) Paul was free to think; yet under an obligation to an authority greater than his own, willing even to contemplate the possibility that he might himself diverge from the true gospel and so incur his own anathema (1.8; cf. 1 Corinthians 9.27). He might seek to please men by his preaching; if he did so he would no longer be the slave of Christ (1.10). It is as Christ's slave that he exercises his theological freedom.

This observation gives us a third characteristic of Paul's theology; it is based on the principle aptly expressed in the words *solus Christus*. Christ alone is his theme. This we shall continue to observe; for the present it suffices to note that, for Paul, Christ is (for example) the criticism of conventional eschatology and the law. The question to be asked of traditional Christian belief and of primitive Christian formulas is whether they do justice to the centrality of Christ. If they do not, they must be changed or developed so that they do. Freedom is not the reward of obligation duly discharged, nor is it an intrinsic human right. Christ alone is freedom: by crucifixion with him I died to law, which is bondage. Christ alone is obligation: I died with him that through him and his resurrection I might live to God (2.19).

FOUR

The Ethics of Obligation:
The Paradox of Ethics

It is at this point that the discussion takes a second turn. You will remember that I pointed out at the beginning that in Galatians three themes, or rather three areas of investigation, could be distinguished – distinguished, but not separated. These were history, theology and ethics. I devoted one chapter to history, and have spent two on theology; I turn now to ethics. Not that we were able to avoid theology in chapter 1, or history in 2 and 3, or allusions to ethics in any of them; similarly we shall soon find ourselves examining afresh the historical situation in Galatia, and all through we shall be looking into the basis of ethics, and for Paul that is certainly theology. We must continue to concern ourselves with the interrelation of these fields. It is only by doing so that we may hope to understand what New Testament Theology is, and only by doing so that we may discover how freedom and obligation may coexist. So far we have heard a good deal about the theology of freedom; we must now turn to look at the other side of the coin.

Immediately we encounter the title I have given to this fourth chapter: 'The Paradox of Ethics'; I should perhaps have called it explicitly the paradox of Christian ethics, or of Pauline ethics. For the very existence of Christian ethics is a paradox; the paradox is nowhere sharper than it is with Paul, and nowhere sharper in Paul than in Galatians. We must remind ourselves of this; it is impossible to underline it too heavily. For Paul, everything turns upon the free action of God in grace; and there is no exception to this 'everything'. It was so in his own conversion. He was firmly committed to the opposite side, a persecutor. That his life was changed was due solely to 'him who called me through his grace' (1.15). Paul had not merited the call, even though it had been determined before his birth by him 'who separated me from my mother's womb' (ibidem). No human merit was involved. It was true that Paul had before his conversion been a diligent observant of the obligation of the law, but that meant only that he had to begin by dying to the law, by counting as loss, as dung, that which

53

previously he had considered to be a credit balance standing in his account (Philippians 3.7f.). He had no credits now; he did not even live, it was Christ, the Christ who had loved him and given himself up to death for him, who lived in him. The same was true of the Galatian Christians before whose eyes he had begun by placarding the loving self-giving Christ. On what ground had they received the Spirit? They knew it was not by works done in obedience to law; they had heard the gospel and received it in faith (3.2); that and nothing more. Their standing as Christians was due wholly and exclusively to the free action of God in grace; nothing else. This determined Paul's actions and his relations with the churches. A different gospel from this, one for example that limited God's freedom and disparaged his grace by insisting on circumcision as a qualification for salvation, was not a gospel at all; it belonged to a different category. Paul was willing to go to Jerusalem to discuss the content of his preaching, ready to recognize that others as well as himself had been entrusted with an apostolate, ready at the same time to recognize the damage they could do to his work if they chose; but he was not willing to compromise the freedom of God to act in grace. This was the cutting edge of that critical theology of which I have spoken, the criterion by which any proposed variant of the gospel must be judged. It might be the old church of Judaism, or the new church of the pillar apostles; it could not be allowed to intervene here. And *sola gratia, sola fide*, remains the criterion by which dogmatics and ecclesiastical polity must be judged still: God by grace justifies the ungodly.

Dogmatics; Christian institutions. But what about ethics? Have we not excluded ethics? Here is the paradox of which I speak. Man's merit contributes nothing to his salvation, which is God's free gift. Therefore, in simple terms, Why be good?

I need not point out that Paul was aware of this problem. It is, as we are about to see, implicit in Galatians. It is explicit in Romans. If it is true that where sin abounds, grace abounds much more, why not produce as much grace as possible, by sinning as much as possible? Shall we continue in sin that grace may abound? Why not? (Romans 6.1). The question will crop up again a few verses later. Since as Christians we are no longer under law (which forbids sin) but under grace (which can be depended on to deal with sin, however grave), why not continue in sin? Why not indeed? (Romans 6.15). Of course Paul answers these questions with a swift 'God forbid', and goes on to explain why he answers them so. But he asked them because they were serious, not trivial questions. He knew that there were those who said that his own teaching was antinomian, and worse. They alleged that he said, 'Let us do evil that good may come,' or at least that that was the logical consequence of what he said (Romans 3.8). But you do not need to be an antinomian to see that there is a serious problem here. Every moral philosophy, every ethical religion, has to answer the question, Why be good? Has not Paul made the question so difficult that it must remain virtually unanswered? More, supposing we allow him to say that we must be good, how is he to answer the question, What does goodness mean? We have seen that law may be regarded as the objectification of morals. If the law is by definition removed, will not morals evaporate into a shapeless vapour, leaving man with no guidance and with no objective values?

Paul does not make the question, the paradox, easy for himself; nor must we. We begin therefore by reminding ourselves of 5.1, which may be regarded as both the end of chapter 4 and the beginning of chapter 5: 'For freedom Christ set us free; so stand fast and do not again become entangled in a yoke of slavery.' The theology of freedom stands out with unmistakable clarity, and probably in a particularly clear image. 'For freedom [or 'with freedom'] Christ set us free' may be an expression whose redundancy is simply intended to give emphasis, but there is still a case (though it has been controverted) for seeing here an allusion to the acts of sacral manumission recorded in many temple inscriptions.[49] A slave was fortunate enough to be able to save money, enough money to purchase himself and thus gain his freedom; but he could not do this because as a slave he did not have the right of purchase. Instead he paid the money into a temple where it was kept by the priests who in the end bought the slave in the name of their god. Thus he acquired a new master; but he was bought, as the inscriptions which gave public notice of the transaction record, τῇ ἐλευθερίᾳ, 'for freedom', in order to be free. Naturally he would avoid, if he could, returning to his old servile status. This allusion is not certain, but it has the advantage of calling to mind Paul's use of ἐξαγοράζειν, 'redeem', in 3.13; 4.5. The thought is not developed; there is nothing here to provide the basis for a detailed doctrine of the atonement, no discussion of the price paid, not even the hint there is in 3.13. Paul's interest is not to develop a theory but to emphasize a practical point: we have already noted the exhortation, 'Do not again become caught up in a yoke of slavery.' As I say, Paul is not (apparently) making it easy for himself to pass over into the realm of ethics.

But there are more ways than one in which true liberty may be lost. Dr H. D. Betz recently made the point very clearly.[50] Liberty may be lost, in the first place, by legalism. We have already heard a good deal about this, and shall hear more. If men make the law their way to heaven they are bound by its chains and lose their freedom. This was happening in Galatia; it was (according to Paul) the message and the achievement of his adversaries the Judaizers. But liberty may also be lost by licence. The man who sets out to express his freedom by following nothing but his own pleasure will find himself bound to himself, the slave of his own lusts and passions. He too has lost his freedom. This is an important observation, and I shall return to it. But we must turn aside to clarify the historical situation presupposed by the epistle.

What is Paul's problem here? Has he not fully dealt with those who were turning the gospel of liberation into a new law, or into the old law? How does the material in chapters 5 and 6 bear on the situation as we have so far seen it? Several answers have been given to this question.

It was with this problem in mind that J. H. Ropes wrote a monograph[51] in which he underlined the question we have already begun to consider. For about four and a half chapters Paul insists in the strongest possible terms on the principle of faith alone. Justification is for the ungodly; no man, however virtuous, can merit salvation; human works, obedience to the law, are of no avail. But from 5.13 onwards he warns his readers against the abuse of freedom. They must not suppose that they are free to do as they like. The warning is not merely negative. The readers are urged to manifest such virtues as love, joy, peace, long-suffering, faithfulness, self-control, and though these are not described as 'works of law' they have a suspiciously similar appearance. The law is summarized (5.14), and obedience to the summary is expected. There is also, it seems, a new law, the law of Christ (6.2), which must be observed, and the consequences of disobedience are serious. God is not mocked; whatever a man sows he will also reap. In other words, behave correctly, or you will come off badly in the judgement.

How is this sudden change of tone to be explained? Following in part W. Lütgert,[52] Ropes suggests that in Galatia Paul was confronted by two sets of opponents. On the one hand, there were the Judaizers, of whom we have already heard enough. They believed that the law provided the only way of salvation. On the other hand stood a group of libertines who taught that so long as you had received the Spirit (and they may here have laid special stress on baptism) nothing else mattered: you could please yourself and do what you liked. We have good reason to think that there were such people in other of Paul's churches. But the upshot in Galatia was that Paul had to fight a war on two fronts, against two sets of enemies. Up to 5.12 he dealt with one, from 5.13 with the other.

Johannes Munck[53] made the surprising suggestion that those who in Galatia were contending for circumcision were not Jews but Gentile Christians. He builds his view on Galatians 6.13, where he insists that the present passive participle (οἱ περιτεμνόμενοι) must be translated not 'the circumcision party' or 'the circumcised' (circumcised from infancy) but 'those who are now, in the present, getting themselves circumcised'. These men do not themselves keep the law – that is, in accordance with Paul's stringent Pharisaic understanding of it; but they wish you, that is, the rest of you Galatians, to be circumcised in order that they may glory in your flesh. Paul himself was in a sense to blame for their attitude. He had taught them to read the Old Testament and to respect it as the word of God. They did so, and found that it enjoined circumcision and, for example, the observance of days, months, seasons and years. They accordingly had themselves circumcised, and pressed the duty upon their fellow Christians in Galatia. At the same time they concluded that since Paul had been silent about this requirement he must be in error, and therefore lacked authority. These newly-circumcised men, though full of enthusiasm for their newly-discovered rite, lacked the moral training that most born Jews had, and naturally took the line that so long as they were circumcised it mattered little how they behaved. Hence Paul has to attack on the one hand their legalism and on the other their licence; thus the two parts of the letter are explained. An interesting opinion; but can we really build so much on the tense of one participle? Is it, indeed, quite impossible to regard the participle as timeless and translate it 'the circumcised'? Would Paul, who did not hesitate to complain of Peter's hypocrisy (2.13), have hesitated to denounce the same fault in Gentiles who had now become propagandists for circumcision? And if they had been arguing for circumcision on the basis of their Old Testament reading would the controversial exegesis of chapters 3 and 4 have been free of any reference to circumcision? I do not think we can follow Munck here.

There is something rather similar in the view of W. Schmithals,[54] though he thinks the opponents were Jews; they were however not Judaizers as this term has usually been understood, but Jewish gnostics. For them, authority rested not on a chain of tradition but on inspiration; they were the 'spiritual men' to whom Paul alludes in 6.1. As gnostics they believed in the cosmic elements, and taught the Galatians to accept their authority as well as that of the law, though of the law they chose only the command of circumcision. Dr Schmithals says that in this they recall the gnostic Cerinthus, who opposed Paul and is said to have been circumcised and kept the Sabbath, while practising immoral conduct. But Cerinthus was not a Jew.

John Bligh,[55] one of the most recent commentators on Galatians, brings severe criticism to bear on all these proposals. His own view is that chapters 5 and 6 are to be interpreted on the lines of the teaching of the Two Ways. This is an ethical scheme with a long history, which goes back to the Old Testament and was still vividly portrayed in the days of our grandfathers in those edifying pictures which showed the courses taken through life by two young men who made their way respectively through Sunday School, Bible Class, Church, devout home life and pious practices to heaven, and through the billiard saloon, the drinking den and the gambling hall to hell. It started, perhaps, in Deuteronomy 11.26–8: 'Behold I set before you this day a blessing and a curse, the blessing if ye shall hearken unto the commandments of the Lord your God, which I command you this day: and the curse, if ye shall not hearken unto the commandments of the Lord your God, but turn aside out of the way that I command you this day, to go after other gods, which ye have not known.'

This pattern of exhortation persisted in Judaism. There is for example a long passage in the Qumran *Manual of Discipline* (3;4):[56]

These are their ways in the world...a spirit of humility, patience, abundant charity, unending goodness, understanding and intelligence; (a spirit of) mighty wisdom which trusts in all the deeds of God and leans on his great loving kindness; a spirit of discernment in every purpose, of zeal for just laws, of holy intent with steadfastness of heart, of great charity...of admirable purity...of humble conduct...And as for the visitation of all who walk in this spirit, it shall be healing, great peace in a long life...a crown of glory and a garment of majesty in unending light.

> But the ways of the spirit of falsehood are these: greed, and slackness in the search for righteousness, wickedness and lies, haughtiness and pride, falsehood and deceit, cruelty and abundant evil, ill temper and much folly and brazen insolence ... so that man walks in all the ways of darkness and guile. And the visitation of all who walk in this spirit shall be a multitude of plagues by the hand of all the destroying angels ... eternal torment and endless disgrace together with shameful extinction in the fire of the dark regions.

It is to be found in the Gospels too.

> Enter in through the narrow gate; for wide is the gate and broad is the path that leads to destruction, and there are many who enter by it; and narrow is the gate and contracted the path that leads to life, and those who find it are few   (Matthew 7.13, 14).

There is also a document common to two early Christian writings, the *Didache* and the *Epistle of Barnabas*. I shall quote some of this beçause it shows how wide of the mark Bligh's suggestion is. This 'Two Ways' document is pure moralism, and shows none of the tension between freedom and obligation that runs through every sentence in Galatians.

> There are two ways, one of life and one of death, and there is much difference between the two ways. The way of life is this: Firstly, thou shalt love God who made thee: secondly, thou shalt love thy neighbour as thyself ... Thou shalt not kill, thou shalt not commit adultery, thou shalt not corrupt boys ... Be not wrathful ... be not an augur ... thou shalt remember him that speaketh to thee the word of God ... Thou shalt confess thy transgressions in the congregation ... This is the way of life. But the way of death is this: first of all it is wicked and full of curse: murders, adulteries, lusts ... grinding down the afflicted, advocates of the rich, unjust judges of the poor, steeped in sin.
> (*Didache* 1.1–5.2)

All this is sound ethical advice, but it is not Paul. It fails to see the paradox of ethics, and takes ethical instruction for granted. I do not think we can accept Bligh's suggestion any more than those of Munck and Schmithals. Ropes may be right, but need not be. There is no reason why Paul should not himself have been aware without external prompting of the two dangers to freedom that I mentioned earlier, nor is there any reason why they should not have been combined in the same persons, or at least why Paul should not have believed that they were combined in the same persons, whom, after all, we know only through his allusions to them. Whether Ropes is right or wrong we are brought back to something like the position of F. C. Baur.[57] I say 'something like' that position, for we learn in this epistle that there was a measure of agreement between Paul and the 'Pillars', James, Cephas and John; and Baur played this agreement down too much. There is however weight in his argument that the Jerusalem apostles, if they had fully agreed with Paul's understanding of the gospel, would have been obliged to join him in his mission to the Gentiles (as, to some extent, Peter did); envoys from James did sow disruption in the church at Antioch; and the Judaizers had some sort of base in Jerusalem. Many of the points made by Käsemann in his study of 2 Corinthians[58] apply equally to Galatians: Paul has to fight his enemies with one hand behind his back because of the difficulties made for him by the Jerusalem authorities, whose half-hearted backing may have been more harmful than downright hostility. This however is a digression from which we must return. Our next task is to explore the paradox of ethics as it unfolds in chapters 5 and 6. But first comes the opening paragraph of chapter 5, which hardly does more than prepare the way for what follows.

We have already looked at the opening verse, but it is so important, and contains so much, that we must spend a little longer on it. The positive assertion at the beginning of the verse is fundamental, but all I need say about it now is that it underlines the *solus Christus* theology that Paul displays throughout. Whether or not we are to see behind Paul's words here an act of redemption by which slaves are bought out from their old servitude into the liberating service of a divine master, there is no mistaking the sole agency of Christ in the process: it was he who set us free, as it was he who loved us and gave himself up for us. The difficulty in the verse does not lie here but in the next clause, and especially in the word 'again'. It is the same problem that we met at 4.9 (pp. 42f.). There, 'the weak and beggarly elements, to which you wish to be enslaved *again*'; here, 'Do not *again* become entangled in a yoke of bondage.' But the Gentile Galatians were not doing, were not being asked to do anything *again*; they were urged to do something they had never done before, to allow themselves to be circumcised and to take on the yoke, or at least part of the yoke, of the Jewish law. No doubt they had been told (cf. 3.3) that to do this would be a step forwards towards perfection: they had begun with faith, let them reach maturity with the law. If Paul's 'again' is justified we have in these two passages as extraordinary a statement as is to be found anywhere in his letters. It is comparable to 1 Corinthians 9.20, where Paul says that to the Jews he became *as if he were* a Jew – *as if he were*, though he had been circumcised the eighth day, belonged to the race of Israel, the tribe of Benjamin, a Hebrew of Hebrews (Philippians 3.5). Here in Galatians he virtually equates Judaism with heathenism. To go forward into Judaism is to go backward into heathenism. As I said when dealing with chapter 4 (p. 42), we have pointers to Paul's meaning in the giving of the law by angels, who might be equivalent to cosmic elements, and in the calendrical aspect of the law – days, months, seasons, years are regulated by the movements of the heavenly bodies. But the main point is that the law, introduced into a fallen world, was not strong enough to stand up to sin, which was already there and in possession of the field. This is hinted at in 3.21: the defect of the law lay not in that which it commanded but in that it had no power to give life. But it is made much clearer and more explicit in Romans 7, especially in verses 10, 13, 23. Sin has the effect of turning law, Torah, the beneficent gift of the good God, into a counterfeit law, sin's law, which becomes man's enemy, takes him prisoner and makes him its slave. It is perhaps unfortunate that Paul in the Greek language had no word corresponding to our 'legalism': it is for this reason tempting to drop the word 'law' and retain 'Torah' for the good use of that good gift of God to men which directs them to himself as the source of life and centre of trust and obedience, 'legalism' for the counterfeit which makes man a slave and ends in his death. But to do this consistently would mean assuming an ability to decide how Paul is using his word (νόμος) on every occasion, and would fail to deal with passages where ambiguity remains. So we retain 'law' as a general term, recognizing its ambiguity.

The passages in Romans 7 to which I have referred show sin transforming good 'Torah' into bad 'legalism'. Sin is personified; such personification of an abstract is mythological, but it is not for that reason unreal. It is easy to see behind it another personalism which is anything but mythological. I may say, and truly, that sin creates legalism; but the sin that affects the transformation, the deformation, of law in my case is my sin; and this means that in truth *I* turn law into legalism by using it as my stepladder, my means of ascent to God's level. It is from this legalism that man is set free by Christ, to this legalism that he must not return, for servitude to the cosmic powers and servitude to the principle of legalism are external and objective, existential and subjective, aspects of the same bondage. We shall come back to this comparison. What we have to note now is that freedom from the law does not mean 'freedom to do as I like'; it means freedom from myself, freedom, that is, to be unselfish, freedom, that is, to live in love. It is not sufficient to say that Paul's theology of freedom is not inconsistent with an ethic of obligation; the two are bound up together. The man who is justified is set free for moral life; but he is justified by grace, through faith, and in Christ only; and as soon as he falls back into a legalistic relation with God he loses his freedom, the freedom to love unselfishly and unselfconsciously.

The verses that follow emphasize this, and the unique significance of Christ. There were probably some in Galatia who thought it would be well to hedge their bets. 'Paul may be right, so we shall certainly not give up Christ' (though it was *another Jesus* that they preached, 2 Corinthians 11.4); they would have been less dangerous had they done so. 'But the Judaizers also may be right, so we will make assurance double sure and add circumcision to our faith in Christ.' It has been the way of the prudent ecclesiastical politician ever since; it takes courage to walk by faith in the invisible Christ, and not to walk by the comforting sight of one's own religious performance. Paul will have none of it. Add something to Christ, and you have lost Christ – not because he is pettishly jealous, but because no man can trust two saviours, no man can walk along two different roads at the same time. Nothing could bring out the *solus Christus* principle more clearly, nothing therefore could make more clearly the point of a *critical* theology. A theology that is content to assert that Christ is a revelation of God, that he presents a way of salvation, that he provides one way into the people of God, is capable of being added to, and lacks any critically exclusive power. But it is good Pauline theology to refuse the offer of a place for Christ in the Pantheon; he stands alone or he stands not at all; even the law of Moses is not to be regarded as a useful or even as a tolerable supplement. So: get yourself circumcised, accept the attractive ecclesiastical compromise, and Christ will do you no good.

Paul is prepared to allow – he does so explicitly in Romans 2 – that justification by law is theoretically possible. He seems not yet (in Galatians) to have seen the further point that he goes on to make in Romans, that it is possible to look back at the law from the vantage point of the Christian's knowledge of Christ and see that the law does bear witness to him and, rightly understood, seeks the same response as the gospel, namely faith. Here, in Galatians, his point (which he never gives up, though he enriches it) is that no one may pick and choose in the law. If you elect to be circumcised you are choosing the way of law, and having chosen it must carry it through: you must, having begun with circumcision, go on to keep the whole law. And the whole law includes, is summed up in, the commandment of perfect love (5.14) – which man does not keep. To observe, for example, the commandment of circumcision, the Sabbath, and the food laws, is possible for anyone; but, given the fall and universal sinfulness throughout the family of Adam, justification by the whole law is not a practical possibility.

Verse 4 repeats the content of verses 2 and 3. Christ is not to be combined with the law as a means of justification. The man who thinks he can justify himself by his own achievement in obedience to the law proclaims thereby that he has no need of grace, and therefore automatically falls out of that relation with God which is defined by grace. The positive counterpart of this is stated with great precision in verse 5. Every word counts and must be duly noted.

We await; that is to say, we do not already possess. The same outlook into the future is shared by the word *hope*. Hope that is seen is not hope (Romans 8.24). Paul never allows his understanding of Christianity to issue in a completely realized enjoyment of salvation; the future dimension is always present.

What we hope for, and confidently expect, is *righteousness*. I have already discussed briefly the meaning of this word. Its primary reference is to the verdict of acquittal in God's court: the positive, self-communicating righteousness with which God acts, the state of righteousness which he confers on the believer, the right relation that exists between him and the pardoned sinner. All this may be presupposed, but two more aspects of the matter arise now. The first may be put in the form of a question. When does Paul expect to receive this righteousness? In the present verse it appears to lie in the future. There is a *hope* of righteousness; we *await* it. I have already made this point. But is not justification, the divine gift of being rightly related to God because acquitted in his court, something that man has already received? Passages in Romans immediately come to mind, such as 5.1: δικαιωθέντες, 'having been justified', having been made right with God. The aorist participle is repeated in the same paragraph (5.9) in contrast with a future: 'Having been justified *now* by his blood we shall be saved ($\sigma\omega\theta\eta\sigma\delta\mu\epsilon\theta\alpha$) through him from wrath', from, that is, the punishment God inflicts upon those not judged righteous in his court. So here the gift of righteousness in justification belongs to the past. But there are also passages in which it seems to belong to the future. We may remain in the same chapter of Romans: at 5.19, 'As through the disobedience of the one man [Adam] the mass of men ($o\acute{\iota}$ $\pi o\lambda\lambda o\acute{\iota}$) were constituted sinners, so through the obedience of the one [Christ] the mass of men shall be constituted ($\kappa\alpha\tau\alpha\sigma\tau\alpha\theta\acute{\eta}\sigma o\nu\tau\alpha\iota$) righteous.' But we are dealing with Galatians; how does Paul speak of righteousness and justification in this epistle?

In a number of passages there is no precise statement of time. Thus at 2.16 the general principle is laid down: a man is not justified by works of law but only by faith in Christ Jesus. The verb is used twice more in this verse, but without a conclusive time reference: 'We became believers in Christ Jesus in order that we might be justified by faith in Christ, for by works of law shall no flesh be justified.' At the end of the chapter (2.21): 'If righteousness comes through the law, Christ died for nothing.' So far we have learned nothing about when righteousness does come. At 3.6 (Genesis 15.6) we learn that Abraham's faith was reckoned ($\dot{\epsilon}\lambda o\gamma\acute{\iota}\sigma\theta\eta$) to him as righteousness; a clear reference to the past. At 3.11 Paul makes another general statement, and so too, in a different way at 3.21. At 5.4 he suggests but does not quite prove a search for righteousness in the present: 'You who would be justified, who think to be justified, by law.'

The ambiguity of these passages is significant. There are two justifications, two acts of acquittal. One is in the present; it is the act, virtually identical with what Paul calls reconciliation, by which God brings the rebel to himself, restores the prodigal to his family. As a result of it we have peace with God, peace given as a free gift of grace. As such it is rightly thought of as the first step in the Christian life, which makes the rest possible; and this is true, for even God must begin by dealing with the sinner as he is since there is no other place where he can begin. But justification is not a first step which the Christian can thereafter put behind him, as an undergraduate puts behind him his matriculation into the university as a step which, once taken, can be forgotten. Justification remains as a dialectical definition of the Christian life at every stage. Man is, as Luther said, *simul justus ac peccator*, a man righteous, as God has made him, but also a man sinful, as he continues to make himself; sinful in himself, righteous by faith. Justification, then, is a beginning, and a process; and it leads to a consummation, at the future judgement, when God's initial gracious verdict on the sinner is – or, it may be, is not – confirmed. The negative possibility is real. Paul is aware of the possibility that he himself may in the end prove to be ἀδόκιμος, rejected, un-approved (1 Corinthians 9.27). He warns his readers that they must all stand before the judgement seat of God, or Christ (Romans 14.10; 2 Corinthians 5.10); and the warning would become a mockery if the result of the judgement were a foregone conclusion. Paul will declare this in Galatians (6.7), and states it elsewhere. He is not contradicting himself; no one can justify himself by his works, but he can de-justify himself and secure his condemnation by his flouting of grace. In other words he can destroy the true freedom he receives by faith by rejecting the obligation this freedom brings with it. So there are not merely two justifications, a present and a future; the two are linked by a process marked at every stage by the principle of justification, and the process is capable of interruption.

The second further aspect of righteousness that must be taken up here arises out of the first and will itself shortly be taken up again. Present treatment of it may therefore be brief. The fundamental meaning of righteousness for Paul is, as I have said, forensic; it has to do with relation rather than with morals. In addition to this primary meaning, however, the word as Paul uses it goes on to collect clear ethical overtones. 'For as in the past you offered your members in servitude to uncleanness and lawlessness, with the result of lawless behaviour, so now offer your members in servitude to righteousness, with the goal of sanctification' (Romans 6.19). This is clear; righteousness means moral rightness. Our verse in Galatians is not so clear, but it shows a movement in this direction. We look for the expression of our new relation to God in observable behaviour.

As we work back through the verse we are reminded that the whole process turns upon faith; justification is not an achievement but the acceptance of a gift. All belongs within the area of covenant, promise and grace that Paul has already marked out; and this is emphasized again, from the other side, by the opening words, 'by the Spirit'. There will be more to say about Paul's use of this word in the next chapter, but already it can be seen that the life of earnest waiting by faith for the hoped for gift of righteousness is actuated by God, by the Spirit; the initiative is God's, not man's. But Spirit is more than this. God's initiative means that he is taking in hand his final acts in putting his world to rights. In a word, Spirit is, in Paul's usage, an eschatological factor, in the sense that the Spirit is the divine agent who begins to bring the future into the present. Most of the evidence for this is to be found in other letters. It will be enough to recall that the Spirit is the *first fruits* (Romans 8.23); not the fullness of God's final harvest but the first sheaves which are at once a part and thereby a promise of the whole. Similarly the Spirit is the *earnest* (2 Corinthians 1.22; 5.5); not the payment in full of all that God has in store for his people, but a substantial deposit, part of the whole and at the same time the pledge that the rest will in due course be paid. The Spirit brings the future into the present. This applies to both the forensic and the moral aspects of righteousness. The final verdict has been anticipated in the verdict of acquittal now received by faith; and this is the Spirit's work. Just as the final verdict at the last day admits to the life, the holiness and the happiness, of the age to come, so justification, as an anticipation of that final verdict, admits to an anticipation of the life, of the holiness and happiness, of the age to come; and this too is the Spirit's work, making it possible for what begins as a matter of relation to appear on the world's stage in ethical behaviour.

This leads to the next step in Paul's argument, which provides the clearest possible combination of freedom and obligation. It can be reached only on the basis we have now discovered in 5.5. The new verse, 5.6, runs: 'For in Christ Jesus neither circumcision avails anything, nor uncircumcision; what does, is faith working through love.'[59] It is now clear that, unless Paul's argument is to be simply discounted, circumcision is totally irrelevant as far as man's existence in the presence of God is concerned. It affects neither man's standing before God nor his own true being. It is a necessary corollary that uncircumcision is equally irrelevant. God does not love and take to himself men either because they are Jews or because they are not Jews. In the given Galatian situation (and there are others where, *mutatis mutandis*, the same observation applies) it is the circumcised who are seeking to impose on others what they regard as their own superior qualifications, not the uncircumcised who are bidding Jews pretend that they are not Jews. In any case, circumcision is in itself an inadequate mark of Judaism, as Paul will argue in more detail in Romans 2. To boast of one's circumcised flesh while withholding the obedience of faith which he requires is to mock God; better never to have been circumcised at all.

What matters is faith working through love. Faith and love must never be confounded with each other; equally they must never be separated. Faith is an openness to God so complete that it can never be combined with the closing of the believer's heart against his fellow. Faith begins as a relation between man and God, but it is a relation which, if it is genuine, has the inevitable result of transforming the believer who exercises it, or is exercised by it, into the image of the one to whom it is directed. Faith includes obedience, and, as we shall shortly see, God commands love. Faith cannot be truly faith if it does not take seriously the command, Thou shalt love thy neighbour as thyself. But faith is more than obedience; it is a confident trust, in which man gives himself up to the one who loved him and gave himself for him. He no longer has any occasion to be concerned about himself, his life in this world or his life in the world to come. So far as he believes he has forgotten himself; and this is a negative definition of love. Thus even obligation becomes an aspect of freedom. The freedom of faith demands and makes possible the obligation of love. Makes possible; there is more to say here, but for the present it will suffice to point forward to it. There is a verse closely parallel to the present one in Galatians 6 (we shall return to it in the next chapter): 'Neither is circumcision anything, nor uncircumcision; what matters is a new creation.' Faith working through love is, as the parallelism shows, the content of the new creation; not man's achievement but God's gift. This will bring us back to the Spirit, but we have not yet reached that point.

At this point Paul plunges back into what has been going on in Galatia, and immediately becomes allusive and difficult. This is inevitable. His readers knew all about what had happened; it would have been a waste of time and possibly counterproductive to describe it. We do not know what had happened; we can only try to reconstruct it from the allusions. Paul uses one of his favourite images. You were running well, making good speed along the track; but someone got in your way. As in 3.1, where he has the same trouble in mind, he is speedily out of the image, for obeying the truth is no metaphor. *The truth* is essentially the gospel; and the Galatians had abandoned it. Things are wrong, and they cannot blame God for it. Looking at other parts of the epistle we may judge that the Judaizers had put it to the Galatians that God was calling them to progress from their original condition as converts to Paul's 'faith only' gospel of freedom to a more advanced gospel, which added the law to the original message. I suspect that in Paul's mind the two clauses belong closely together. The Galatians are not obeying (μὴ πείθεσθαι) the truth. The kind of obedience into which you have been persuaded (ἡ πεισμονή) does not come from God. The two words stand side by side.

There follows in 5.9 a familiar proverb, which Paul uses again at 1 Corinthians 5.6. A little leaven leavens the whole lump; behind this metaphorical use of leaven as a source of taint or evil lies the Passover law which required that all leaven, all fermenting material (ḥameṣ) should be removed from a house before Passover was celebrated. Does the image ('a little leaven') imply that things had not yet gone far wrong in Galatia, that only a few were so far infected? It would be rash in view of verses such as 4.20b, and the general tone of the letter, to infer this. If we can reconstruct any Galatian history from the verse, we might guess that only a few intruders had come into the church from outside. This finds some confirmation in the next verse. As regards the community as a whole Paul was confident; was he really? Is he using tact? He continues in the singular: 'Only he who is troubling you shall bear his judgement, be he who he may' (5.10). I mentioned this verse in the first chapter. Who was 'he who is troubling you'? How was he related to 'those who are troubling you' (1.7; 5.12)? What is the significance of ὅστις ἐὰν ᾖ, whoever he may be? This reminds us again of an earlier verse, 2.6: ὁποῖοί ποτε ἦσαν οὐδέν μοι διαφέρει, 'whatever they were makes no difference to me.'[60] The meaning is the same; there it is related to the pillar apostles in Jerusalem. There are two main possibilities. One is that Galatia had been invaded by a group of people, who had a ringleader. The other is that behind the invaders stood a more remote figure – James, from whom had come those who caused such disturbance in the church of Antioch.[61] There are many interesting inferences to be drawn here regarding the early history of Christianity, but we cannot pursue them now.

The next verse is one of the greatest puzzles in the epistle. Did someone allege that Paul – of all men – was preaching circumcision? Would not the allegation be thought ridiculous, so ridiculous that Paul would have no need to counter it? We can only say that he presumably did not think when he wrote this verse that he was wasting ink. So he was still being persecuted; why *still*? I can only think that this means, After the Council described in chapter 2. Before then it was alleged that he was perverting both

Judaism and Christianity by teaching that men might become members of the people of God without circumcision. It is interesting that we have little evidence of the persecution of Paul on this account at this time. There is some in Acts 9, but its value is doubtful. For example, Luke alleges that it was a Jewish plot that led to Paul's escape from Damascus in a basket, but Paul himself, who must have known the facts, says that it was the Ethnarch of the Arab Aretas who was trying to seize him. No doubt however the Jews would be enraged by the conversion – defection as it must have seemed to them – of their most earnest and active advocate. There is plenty of evidence, probably belonging to the later time, of persecution by 'false brothers', that is, Judaizing Christians (2 Corinthians 11.26). So *still*, after the Council which was supposed to bring peace to the Church, Paul was being persecuted. This, he says, disproves the proposition that he still preached circumcision. There was no point in saying this if the allegation was not made. It is the opposite of the charge brought in Acts 21.21. It is however possible that we should see in the manoeuvres described in that chapter not a direct attack on Paul so much as an attempt to drive a wedge between him and his Gentile churches. A whisper that he did himself preach circumcision – when it suited him to do so – might contribute to the process. Such a story could be based on exaggeration of 1 Corinthians 7.18; or possibly on Paul's circumcision of Timothy (or on the report, whether true or false, that he had circumcised him, Acts 16.3); or on the circumcision of Titus (if Titus was circumcised, Galatians 2.3); or indeed on nothing at all but malice (Paul knew what it was to be slandered, Romans 3.8).

Men persecute when they are offended, scandalized – σκανδαλίζονται. And they are offended by the cross; but this offence could have been done away by accepting the requirement of circumcision. You cannot preach both the cross and circumcision, for the cross is the enemy of all the rites and institutions to which men cling for salvation, in which they suppose they can make their salvation secure. It is circumcision as security, not as for example a national custom, that Paul opposes. And the cross is the denial of all security. It is those only who take up the cross and follow in the steps of Christ who find justification in him. The man who hangs on the cross has surrendered every kind of human security, and those who follow him must surrender it too. There is nothing so wounding as this to man's pride.

Are we to end this chapter with a nasty taste in the mouth?

What are we to make of 5.12? It is often taken to be a witticism of Paul's;[62] if it was, it was in very bad taste and there is no defending it. 'I would that those who are upsetting you (by demanding that you be circumcised) would castrate themselves' – as the priests of Cybele, for example, did. But I do not think this was intended as a joke, and I am not sure that the verse is rightly translated. If the translation is correct, a serious theological point is involved. Circumcision (so its advocates urged) was a necessary qualification for membership of the people of God; castration was a disqualification. So that (if there is a reference to castration) Paul would be saying: 'I wish those people who want to qualify you for membership would disqualify themselves.' But I am not quite sure that AV's rendering, 'cut themselves off', is wrong.

Whatever be the meaning of this verse, Paul has now laid the foundations for his concluding argument, showing that there is no conflict but rather an indissoluble union between the theology of freedom and the ethics of obligation. Nor is there any question of a compromise between the two in which each is watered down so as to accommodate the other. Freedom is real freedom, and any attempt to restrict it must be firmly refuted. But obligation is real obligation too, and there must be no attempt to evade it.

FIVE

The Ethics of Obligation:
Flesh and Spirit

So there is no contradiction between freedom and obligation. There is no conflict between faith and love; faith expresses itself in love. Anything that does not work itself out in love, though it may conceivably be verbal orthodoxy, is not faith in Paul's sense of the term. The historical meaning of the *auto-da-fé* is an internal contradiction; Pauline faith does not issue in the burning or torturing of a fellow man, though it may well have to tell him, and tell him sharply, that he is in error. There is no conflict but a necessary connection between faith and love; but that does not mean that there is no conflict at all. Christian ethics rests upon an absolute obligation, and freedom must not be allowed to become licence. The freedom of faith must not be destroyed by legalism; this point Paul has laboured throughout the epistle and he has not finished with it yet. The freedom of faith must not be corrupted by licence; to this point he now turns, and here he discloses the conflict that lies at the heart of Christian existence.

First (5.13) he reiterates the basic freedom of a Christian: 'You were called for freedom, brothers.' Then he continues: 'Only do not allow your freedom to become an opportunity for the flesh.' So the *flesh* is the danger; this is what may, if permitted, abuse freedom. This is the enemy that must be fought. But what does Paul mean by 'flesh'? It has sometimes been taken in a very literal sense to mean the material side of man's existence, with the implication that we can live as God intends only by constant mortification of the flesh, by living in pain, discomfort, hunger. Often this interpretation has been given a special turn in relation to man's sexual desires and activities. Fight against the flesh by observing poverty, chastity and obedience; only those who do so achieve the fullness of the Christian life. Few would, I think, today maintain this in a crude form. It is possible to be a Christian outside the cloister. But most modern translations of the Bible use some kind of paraphrase. The *New English Bible*, for example, translates 'our lower nature', a most unfortunate rendering, not least because it implies that we have a higher nature which if left

71

to itself would be intrinsically good; Paul knows no such higher nature. The *Good News Bible* has 'your physical desires', which is perhaps worse, and seems to return to the old, and quite un-Pauline, condemnation of sex. The *Jerusalem Bible* does much better with 'self-indulgence', but this is a rendering that cannot be carried through for every occurrence of the word. It seems to me that translators should be content to do what Paul did. He used a simple Greek word, σάρξ, which simply means 'flesh'. Of course his thought was not confined to that material substance of which, along with bones, blood and so forth, our bodies are composed; but what he meant more than this he left his readers to find out as they considered the contexts in which he used the word. A commentator will naturally do more, but a translator should be content to say 'flesh' and leave the reader to put the various passages together. Certainly there are difficulties in doing this, for Paul did not always write with the pernickety care of a professional theologian. Thus at Romans 8.9 he writes, 'You are not *in flesh* but in Spirit, if the Spirit of God dwells in you.' This is certainly descriptive of the Christian, of every Christian, for Paul goes on, 'If any man does not have the Spirit of Christ he does not belong to Christ.' Very well then; the Christian is not 'in flesh'. But we recall Galatians 2.20, where Paul says, 'The life I now live *in flesh* I live by faith in the Son of God who loved me and gave himself for me.' Here speaks a Christian, if ever there was one; and he now as a Christian lives 'in flesh'. There is no escape from the conclusion that Paul's language is inconsistent, but the inconsistency lies simply in his use of prepositions. In the passage in Romans 8 he should have written, as he does elsewhere, 'according to flesh' (κατά, not ἐν). The Christian lives 'in' flesh for he has no choice in the matter, but he is not governed, controlled, by flesh.

So, with due caution, we proceed to examine what Paul says. *Flesh* is active, ready to seize an opportunity if one is presented to it. In this it is like *sin* (Romans 7.11), and undoubtedly there is a close connection between the two. Flesh is a positive force for evil, and it will take advantage of Christian freedom if it can. It waits to see what you will do with your freedom, to influence what you will do with your freedom. What it is becomes clear through the opposite which stands over against it. You are not to use your freedom as an opportunity for the flesh; but, on the contrary, through love serve one another. The opposite of flesh is love; and love means serving one another. This becomes clearer still as Paul goes on (5.14) to quote the commandment of love for the neighbour. Flesh, therefore, defined by its opposite, means self-centred existence, egocentric existence; not specifically a proclivity to carnal sins (as we call them), but a concern focused upon oneself – the *Jerusalem Bible's* 'self-indulgence', perhaps, except that this suggests indulgence in material pleasures, whereas for Paul 'flesh' can express itself in non-material, indeed in religious ways. Again, completing the circle, we see from a different angle how faith and love cohere. Each has equally turned away from self; faith looks away from the self and its achievements to God as the centre of its trust; love looks away from the self and its wishes, even its real needs, to the neighbour, and spends its resources on his needs.

This love, this service of the 'other', is what the law requires. Paul who asserts man's freedom from the law never thinks of proclaiming his independence of God. Man, especially the Christian, owes God obedience, and the law proves after all to provide the channel through which that obedience is to be directed. We recall 3.21: the law does command what is right; it does make known what God requires; all it lacks is the power to give life. Does this mean that Paul, having made a great show of throwing out the law through the front door, now proceeds unobtrusively to readmit it through the back? We could put this question in another way. Paul sums up the law in the command that man should love his neighbour; presumably then, since the whole law is summed up in this one saying, a man who has fulfilled this one precept has done what God requires of him. But Paul had objected (5.3) when the Judaizers had picked out one precept and made it stand for all. They said, 'You must be circumcised, but this one grand precept of the law will cover all the rest.' It is this attitude Paul has in mind when he says, 'I testify again to every man who is being circumcised that he is under obligation to do the whole law'; that is you cannot abstract one command and say that that sums up the total requirement of the law. What is the difference? Why is Paul allowed to sum up the law under one head when the Judaizer is not? What is the difference between the two choices? One answer to this question presents itself immediately: Jesus had already made the same selection from the Torah (Mark 12.31). It is the more surprising that neither here nor in Romans 13.8–10, where he uses very similar words, does Paul acknowledge any indebtedness to Jesus or claim his authority for what he says. It is also true that Jesus himself was not the first Jew to see the meaning of the law in the love that can do its neighbour no harm.[63] It is easy also to observe that circumcision is a ritual law and love a moral requirement; but Paul does not point this out nor does he elsewhere make much of the distinction, and it is necessary to take a further step beyond this observation. Circumcision is the sort of thing which, if abstracted from the rest of the law, can be performed as an end in itself; indeed it can hardly be performed in any other way. Love, on the other hand, if it is rightly understood, cannot be performed as an end in itself; the moment it becomes such an end it ceases to be disinterested love – that is, it ceases to be love. This means that the law of circumcision, if it is taken on its own, inevitably becomes not law but legalism; the law of love cannot become legalism but rather acts as a safeguard against legalism.

There is probably a pointed glance at the Galatian communities when Paul goes on to observe (5.15) that the end of non-love is mutual destruction. No common life is possible when all the individual components are centred upon themselves; they will simply devour one another.

So *flesh* stands over against *love*, and love therefore goes a long way towards explaining what flesh is; flesh is love with a minus sign placed outside the bracket, reversing all the signs within. But Paul now finds a new counterpart to flesh. 'Walk by the Spirit and you will not fulfil the desire of the flesh' (5.16). If flesh is taken to mean 'our lower nature' we shall be inclined to take Spirit to mean our higher nature; but this is not Paul's common use of the word. Why does he use it here? Perhaps (so some have suggested) because his opponents, or one group of his opponents, made much of the gifts of the Spirit; they were the spiritual men of 6.1. This may have contributed to Paul's reasons for referring to Spirit, but only marginally. It would not account for the frequent references to Spirit over against flesh in Romans 8.1–11. The Spirit is referred to here because it is the second necessary counterpart to flesh. Love is its ethical counterpart, Spirit its theological counterpart. Love, as we have seen, can be clumsily defined as non-self-centred existence. But man cannot by a simple decision of his own reverse his own egocentricity. His attempts to do so issue in the many man-centred forms of religious and philosophical thought. It has been said that the proper theological version of the famous saying of Descartes, '*cogito, ergo sum*', is '*cogitat, ergo sum*'; that is, my being depends not on my thought but on God's thought of me. This may or may not be true in general metaphysics. It is true in respect of Christian ethics in the sense that if man's life is to be centred no longer on man himself it will need a new centre, and the divine centre available to reconstruct human life as the basis and for the practice of love is what Paul means by Spirit, the divine activity by which the love of God is shed abroad in our hearts. With Paul, Spirit (πνεῦμα) has not yet become explicitly the third person of the Trinity, though there are passages (notably 2 Corinthians 13.13) that look in that direction, and the non-human centre of human life transformed into the image of divine love, if read against the Old Testament background, would be a not insignificant step.

It is worth observing that Paul is saying something different from what the Qumran manuscripts mean by the spirit of truth and the spirit of error, or by spirit and flesh. Differences as well as a few resemblances have been brought out in detail by W. D. Davies,[64] but the principal contrasts are two. In the first place, for Paul flesh does not stand for some kind of angelic being outside man, who attacks him and impels him willy-nilly in the direction of evil; it is man himself, man who has chosen to be left to himself, man's *cor incurvatum in se* (to use Luther's vivid phrase). Man cannot, in Paul's view, look outside himself and blame his wrong-doing on a being called *flesh*, other than himself. In the second place, as W. D. Davies points out, in the Qumran literature Spirit lacks the eschatological connection that we have already seen to be central in Paul's understanding of it.

Paul's 'flesh' is much nearer to the rabbinic notion of the *yeṣer*, the inclination or tendency within man that drives him to do evil. Paradoxically, the parallel is to be found in the fact that the rabbis insisted that the *yeṣer* was in a sense good – were it not so God could not have made it. Without it men would not marry, have children, build cities; in a word, civilization would not exist. In this sense it goes back to the initial charge to man in creation: 'Be fruitful, and multiply, and replenish the earth, and subdue it; and have dominion over the fish of the sea, and over the fowl of the air, and over every living thing that moveth upon the earth' (Genesis 1.28). So sex is not in itself evil; man's rule over nature is not in itself evil; but each carries within itself the possibility of abuse, when man exercises his sexual capabilities with a view simply to self-gratification, and without love, and when he exercises power over other beings, human or subhuman, out of sheer will to power, and without love. The *yeṣer* is, broadly speaking, man's potential, thus applied; God made it, and it was good, man abused it, and the end product was evil. Similarly for Paul, 'flesh' is man, and he may so live in the flesh by faith that Christ lives within him. But outside Christ, flesh exists in and for itself, and this means man-centred, self-centred life; and there is always the peril that this kind of living may take control of and abuse even Christian freedom. Flesh, as God's creation, could and should be good, but it has in fact – Paul would doubtless have said, from the time of Adam, that is, universally – changed sides, gone sour. An Old Testament text, often quoted and often misinterpreted, is Isaiah 31.3: 'The Egyptians are men, and not God; and their horses are flesh, and not spirit.' There is nothing wrong in this; you cannot blame the horses for being made of flesh any more than you can blame the Egyptians for being men, which they were created to be, and not God, which they were never intended to be. What is wrong is that the people of God, as appears from the whole context in Isaiah, are putting their trust in the wrong place, in the Egyptian cavalry rather than in God.

It follows from this (and we shall see it confirmed as we proceed) that those renderings of 'flesh' that I quoted earlier – 'our lower nature', 'self-indulgence', and especially 'your physical desires' – may be completely misleading. 'Flesh' (as Paul understands it) may lead to drunkenness or sexual promiscuity; it may also lead, for example, to overbearing prelacy, in which one Christian gains rights or power over another and imposes his will because it is his will and he likes to have his own way and exercise power. Christian freedom presents a special set of temptations, most of all if I forget that he who made me free has made by brother free with the same freedom. For flesh (in the Pauline sense) there is but one cure: Spirit – understood also in the Pauline sense of the power of Christ operative and central in the life of man.

Flesh and *Spirit* then are opposites. They pull in opposite directions, 'that you may not do the things you wish' (5.17). Luther recalling Romans 7 – 'The good I would, I do not; the evil that I would not, that I practise' – took this to mean, 'that you may not do the good things you wish to do'. You will never shake off the flesh; you will never be able to move smoothly ahead, achieving all the good things you mean to do. This is true, but it is not the whole truth. 'The things you wish to do', you being the man that you are, may well be bad things; and the Spirit is at work to prevent you from doing them. The result is doubtless a mixture of good and evil, but there is fruit of the Spirit as well as works of the flesh.

There is no need to work through the two lists. As far as the works of the flesh (5.19–21) are concerned, the thing to note is that they are not all what we should describe as carnal sins. Some are: fornication, uncleanness, lasciviousness, drunkenness, revellings. And the sexual sins stand first because they are the clearest of all examples of a man, or woman, arrogating to himself rights he does not possess, exploiting for his own indulgence not only another's property but another's person, and at its most sensitive point. But idolatry, sorcery, enmities, strifes, jealousies, wrath, factions, divisions, party spirit, envyings, these too are works of the flesh; and church history has been and is littered with them. Not all are carnal sins, but all are self-centred sins. They underline the fact that sin is egocentricity; and the flesh is man's innate tendency to egocentricity. 'Richard loves Richard; that is, I am I.'[65] Self-love is bound up with self-awareness, with personality. Of ourselves we cannot escape it. Those who practise such things will not inherit God's kingdom (5.21). Of course not; they are not heirs because they do not belong to Christ (3.29), and they do no belong to Christ because they insist on belonging to themselves.

If Paul had headed his second list (5.22, 23) 'works of the Spirit' it would not only have led to a clash with 'works of law', it would have been positively misleading. Paul's use of 'works' ($\xi\rho\gamma\alpha$) suggests works that men do, and these are not human products but the result of God's Spirit's dwelling within men. Inevitably, the first word in the list is *love*, and Paul might well have contented himself with that word alone. Many of those that follow are special manifestations of love: long-suffering, kindness, goodness, faithfulness, meekness, and the others are not far removed: joy, peace, self-control. All are the consequence of the self-forgetfulness that looks away from itself to God. The Spirit which affects this disregard of self is in no sense legal, still less legalistic; yet in its effect it is entirely moral. This explains the *ad hominem* dig with which Paul winds up his list. 'You want to observe the law, don't you? You will not find any law that forbids these things' (5.23).

It is those who belong to Christ who thus manifest the fruit of the Spirit; they (over against those who produce the works of the flesh) are heirs and will inherit the kingdom of God. Belonging to Christ means belonging to the only Christ there is, that is, to Christ crucified, and, as Paul will bring out more fully when he writes Romans, belonging to Christ crucified means dying with him, sharing the death that he died, that is, a death to sin (Romans 6.10). Here Paul puts it in a different way, saying that those who belong to Christ have crucified the flesh along with its passions and desires. It matters little which way round the expression runs: dead to sin, or having put the flesh to death. In any case Paul's absolute statement here must be read in the light of 5.13. There is a sense in which the flesh has been crucified, but there is another in which it is still very much alive and looking out for its opportunity to abuse not only natural but Christian freedom.

The epistle is moving to its close, but there is still material of great importance for our theme – which after all is not so much our theme as the theme of the epistle. I have quoted (p. 56) H. D. Betz's acute observation that there are two ways in which Christian freedom may be lost; it may be lost through legalism, or through licence. There is also a third way through which it may be lost. There are those who turn Christianity into emotional, ecstatic, 'charismatic' inspiration, and have no regard to Christian ethics. We are again touching upon affairs in Galatia, and again, since Paul does not need to describe them for the benefit of the Galatians and was not writing for ours, we have to pick up what hints we can find in the absence of explicit statements. But how are we to understand 5.25 if it does not mean that there were in Galatia those who would reply to what Paul had said about flesh and Spirit with the excited response: 'Yes, we live by the Spirit. All that you said from chapter 3 onward is true. We received the Spirit, we work miracles, we prophesy, we speak with tongues.' Paul, if we may judge from the Corinthian correspondence as well as from the present passage, would not chide them – not yet. But he has something to add. 'If we live by the Spirit let us see to it that our lives conform to the Spirit, who is the Spirit of Christ.' There is something wrong with a person who speaks with tongues but shows no love, or joy, or peace, who does not have the love of God shed abroad in his heart. The danger of the charismatic has always been – and I neither say nor imply that all, or many, charismatics fall into it – that he uses the divine gifts as a means of self-aggrandizement, a means of advertising his own self-importance; and this is contrary to the effect of 'de-ego-centrification' that is the work of the Spirit.

I said that Paul does not begin by chiding the inspired men of Galatia, but he goes on to what seems to imply a grim picture of the churches. Is 5.26 simply a warning of what conceivably might happen? Is it a statement of general principles, or a picture of what was already happening? Were some boasting of their circumcision? of their spiritual gifts? Did those who had these gifts provoke others to imitate them? Did those who did not have them envy those who had? It is easy to ask questions, impossible to answer them with any confidence. But it may be said that Galatians does not look like an essay expressing general truths. Almost all of it is plainly and passionately addressed to circumstances that obtained in Galatia. This means (I think) that the odds are that here too Paul was dealing with what he knew, or believed, to be happening in Galatia; and the next verse, like the preceding one, suggests a context of spiritual gifts rather than, at this point, one of Judaizing.

For 6.1 addresses the spiritual people, οἱ πνευματικοί. This is not one of Paul's common terms for the community as a whole, and I think it probable that he uses it to denote a group who claimed the title for themselves. It is their Christian duty not to congratulate themselves on their own spirituality, nor to cut out an unworthy member, but to restore him to the fold. Again one asks whether there is a general or a particular reference. Some have seen an allusion to Peter and his error at Antioch; but 2.11–14 seems impossibly remote. Again, we can only guess, but Christian men do fall into sin and when they do must be restored, and in the right way. Even the spiritual, not least the self-styled spiritual, are not secure; Paul knew that he was not (1 Corinthians 9.27). Discipline must therefore be exercised in meekness. Paul had no love for excommunication, and as a rule was ready to wait in hope that an offender would come to a better mind. There is a striking similarity here to the measures provided for the restoration of an offender in Matthew 18.15; but again Paul shows no sign of an awareness that he is drawing on the teaching of Jesus. He also shows no sign that he knows of any kind of hierarchical government of the churches in Galatia. If 'the spiritual' are not the Christian body as a whole, charged by Paul with the task of restoring an offender, they are a group who have no hierarchical but a purely religious distinction (and that possibly mentioned by Paul with a measure of irony). If 'the spiritual' are the Galatian church as a whole then clearly the whole church is expected to share in the disciplinary process. In neither case does Paul himself expect to take part in it.

'Bear one another's burdens' (6.2) has a specific application in this context, and Paul's understanding of the way a Christian group should conduct its affairs becomes particularly clear. You should be more ready to help your stumbling brother than to condemn and expel him. And the action is reciprocal; no privileged group stands out from the rest.

To bear one another's burdens is to fulfil the law of Christ. We have heard in this letter a good deal about law of one kind and another. What is the 'law of Christ'? Is this a new law, comparable with the law of Moses, but more exacting, Moses raised to a higher degree? If so, to whom does it apply? Are Christians, freed from the old law, now bound to a new one of greater stringency? Does it mean the new exposition and application of the old law expected in the Messianic Age? In this case 'Christ' will be not a name but a title: the Torah of the Messiah. Does it refer to a collection of the teaching of Jesus, such as, for example, the Sermon on the Mount? Or does Paul here, after all, show that he is aware of the fact (unnoticed at 5.14) that Jesus had picked Leviticus 19.18, 'Thou shalt love thy neighbour as thyself', out of the Torah as the one commandment that included and summarized all? The words themselves, 'the law of Christ', do not enable us to answer all these questions, though we may note as we proceed that the phrase occurs nowhere else in Paul's writings. Some have seen an allusion to it in 1 Corinthians 9.21 (Paul is Christ's obedient – law-abiding – one), but it is probably nearer to the truth to say that there Paul is careful to avoid using it, thinking perhaps that it might be misunderstood. The phrase can be understood only from the context, and we must return to it when we have looked at the context; it seems, however, reasonable to say that if Paul was saying that those whom he had rescued from the law of Moses were now to be subjected to a more rigorous law he was writing nonsense, and that bearing one another's burdens, in which he sees the law of Christ fulfilled, is not unrelated to the love of one's neighbour.

'If anyone thinks himself to be something when he is nothing he deceives himself' (6.3). If this is a purely general statement it is so obvious and trite as to be ridiculous, as ridiculous as saying, 'If anyone thinks cows to be identical with sheep he is making a mistake.' There must be a specific reference if Paul is to retain any reputation for intelligence. But what? We have only one pointer, and that may be misleading. The word for thinking oneself to be something is δοκεῖν. This verb was used of James, Cephas and John at 2.6, 9. These verses are usually translated, 'who were reputed to be something' (τῶν δοκούντων εἶναί τι), 'those reputed to be pillars' (οἱ δοκοῦντες στῦλοι εἶναι). It is quite possible that the verb should be translated in chapter 2 in the way that it must be translated in chapter 6: 'James, Cephas and John, who thought themselves to be something, who thought themselves to be pillars'. Paul would then, at the close of the epistle, be returning to the irony he used at the beginning. The Jerusalem apostles may have a high opinion of themselves, but if they have they are deceiving themselves. The more I study the relations between Paul and Jerusalem the more likely it seems to me that this is what he means. It corresponds precisely with the irony he uses in 2 Corinthians 11.5; 12.11 when speaking of the 'superapostles'. The allusiveness of the verse shows the difficulty in which Paul finds himself. He is surrounded by bitter enemies, out to destroy his work, who trade on their connection with Jerusalem and seem to claim the backing of the original apostles. Yet these original apostles have recognized Paul, accepted his gospel, and acknowledged his mission to the Gentiles. What can he say about them? Well, he can make general statements such as this one, and anyone who sees where he thinks the cap will fit can do with it what he pleases. It is to be feared that there were and always have been in the Church too many heads that the cap has fitted all too well. In Galatia we may think of Judaizers who boasted (as Paul had done in the past) that they, unlike mere proselytes, had been circumcised the eighth day; of ecstatics who thought that their spiritual gifts elevated them to a superior level and gave them a right to look down on less fortunate and well-endowed fellow Christians; of ministers who in virtue of their position lorded it over the flock entrusted to them and supposed that their office put them in the position of master. Of course Jews, with the privileges of Israel behind them, charismatics, whose service is due wholly to the working of the Spirit of God, ministers who can never be lords but only the slaves of their people, should know better than others that they are in truth – nothing; only instruments in the hand of God.

Paul has been envisaging a situation in which men are always looking over their shoulders at others and thinking how much better work they themselves do; but this is not bearing one another's burdens. It is not for me to judge someone else's servant (Romans 14.4); that is a task for the other man's master. It is for me to test my work, not his; in this way I have something of my own to boast about. Each has a responsibility for others, but he has no right to impose himself on others. There is no contradiction between verse 5 and verse 2. I must bear up the burdens that weigh my fellows down, but I cannot look to anyone else to bear my responsibilities. Paul has no love for a hierarchy. In his churches all Christians are equal, and all share in responsibility for the good of the whole.

All are equal; but it may be right to add that some are more equal than others. For example, there will always be those who teach, and those who are content to be taught. It is interesting to note here what may be the earliest reference to any kind of paid Christian ministry. Those who taught the word, if their work is to be distinguished from Paul's mission preaching, presumably taught and explained such summaries of Christian belief as occur in 1 Corinthians 15.3–5. They were rewarded for their work, though not, it seems, with a regular salary but by spontaneous sharing on the part of the person being instructed. It is of course probable that the teachers would hold secular posts and teach new converts in their spare time. It would be interesting to know if any of them worked as secular teachers, and if so what they made of non-Christian philosophy and religion.

Again Paul turns to the Galatian situation and makes allusions that we cannot track down; for it does not seem likely that it was simply his reference to the teacher's reward that led him to the thought of the rewards, good and ill, that God would some day distribute. There were some, then, who thought they could mock God and get away with it. What they were doing we can only guess. Paul may have had in mind perversion of truth by those who preached a different gospel; or the antinomianism that forgot God's requirement of love, either in the enthusiasm of a law-free gospel or in the ecstatic enjoyment of spiritual gifts. Paul does not forget that there is a judgement to come. It is not easy to combine the two justifications (pp. 63–5), the one to be had now by faith, the other to come only at the last day when all men give to God an account of their actions; but to ignore the one is to fall into legalism, to ignore the other is to fall into antinomian presumption, and it is better to give up the intellectual puzzle and set the two side by side than to fall into either of these errors. So we keep on doing that which is good, working out the consequences of justification and expressing faith in love, so exercising freedom as to give no opportunity to the flesh.[66]

It may be that Paul had a particular complaint to make against the Galatian churches. We know from 1 Corinthians 16.1 that Paul was at work in Galatia on his collection for the poor saints in Jerusalem. Perhaps the Galatians had not been as generous as he thought they ought to have been. It is verse 10, with its reference to members of the household of faith, that suggests this possibility. Paul has been accused on the basis of this verse of narrowing the conception of Christian love. Jesus had bidden men to love not only their friends (as the publicans do) but their enemies too; Paul if he does not confine Christian love and service to one's fellow believers appears to give them first place. But John Bligh[67] has suggested that the 'members of the household of faith' are, or include, the Jerusalem Christians — the very people who were attacking Paul's person, contradicting his gospel, and threatening to destroy his churches. If he was making a special appeal for them this was love for enemies indeed! It seems that Paul did think of his collection as not merely an act of charity but as a means of Christian unity and of furthering the gospel among Jews.

We come to the end of the paragraph and return to the question what Paul meant by 'the law of Christ'. I see in this paragraph no signs of a code. The whole of 6.1–10 is incidental and *ad hoc*. Paul turns from one thing to another as various pieces of information from Galatia come into his mind. Some of his remarks are quite specific; for example, teachers should be respected and recompensed by those whom they teach. Some may be specific, though we are now too ill informed to perceive what they are specific about. Others are completely and intentionally general. The way of the flesh, that is, of life that is centred upon itself, is death; the way of the Spirit, that is, of life that is centred upon God, is the eternal life of God himself. The 'law of Christ' as the term is used in 6.2 is virtually indistinguishable from the law of love in 5.14. There is no reason to regard it as a technical term. It is named the law of Christ either because Paul did have some reason to think (though he does not tell us so) that Jesus had pointed it out, or, perhaps less probably, because it summed up what he knew of the life and teaching of Jesus.

This brings us to the last paragraph of the letter, in which Paul looks back over the whole of what he has written: a good summary for him, and a good concluding summary for us too, not only because of its contents but because it provides good ground for picking up what I said at the beginning (pp. 3, 4) about the interpenetration of history, theology and ethics, and therewith the interrelation between freedom and obligation. There is history in verses 12, 13, where Paul again denotes (but does not name) those who are unsettling and perverting the Galatian churches, and again in verse 17, in a piece of allusive autobiography. There is theology — theology indeed all through, but especially in verses 14, 15. And there is ethics too, in verses 14, 15, where it is inseparable from the theology, and in verse 16, where — surprisingly, perhaps — Paul speaks of conformity to a rule. What he means by this we shall have to consider. The autobiography of verse 17 has general as well as personal ethical overtones. In this paragraph, as Erasmus said, Paul talks 'pure flame', but there are reasons and logic behind and within his incandescence.

He starts with a banner headline, or, perhaps better, a note that the whole is to be printed in heavy type. Up to this point he has been content to dictate the letter; this was evidently his usual practice. But he cannot end without himself putting pen to paper. The suggestion that his sight was defective and that he was therefore obliged to write a large and flowing hand is one of the unintentional jokes of New Testament criticism. His big writing is part of the placarding of Christ crucified (3.1). Look, you dear Galatian fools, he says; whatever you may leave out don't omit this or pretend that you can't see it.

Was Paul fair to his opponents? 'Those who wish to show well in the flesh, they it is who are trying to compel you to be circumcised; and they do it only in order to avoid being persecuted on account of the cross of Christ' (6.12). We shall come back to the question whether Paul was fair; there are other things to look at on the way. We must assume that the essence of the Galatian situation was that certain persons were insisting that Gentile converts to Christianity must be circumcised. Verse 13 as well as 5.3 suggests that they picked out this commandment and were at least less insistent on other legal requirements. Acts 15.1 confirms the tradition that there were groups in the early Church that did take this line, though it is to be noted that Acts 15.5 adds the rest of the law, and it is not impossible that it was Paul himself who selected circumcision as the requirement most likely to be repulsive to Gentiles. But what of their motivation? Paul ascribes two motives to them; neither of these appears to be an honest conviction that circumcision was a requirement laid down by God for all who would belong to his people.

First, they wish to make a good show in the flesh; with this we may put verse 13b – 'they wish to glory in your flesh'. The word 'flesh' in these two verses must have its simple, literal sense, though it may have a theological sense too. The process on which the Judaizers insist is a surgical operation performed on human bodies. So much is clear. But beyond this, they wish to have something to show, a visible sign; and they wish to have such a sign as will manifest their authority over the persons concerned. These are motives that cohere with the meaning of 'flesh' that we have already examined, and they are of much wider significance than the original Galatian context. Throughout Christian history we may see men actuated by the desire to trust in something, to trust in anything, rather than the mere mercy and grace of God. Man likes to have what Paul in Philippians 3 described as his credit balance, and is instinctively unwilling to do as Paul did when he shifted his credits to the other side of the balance sheet and regarded them as debits. He likes moreover to have his credits in visible form, to be able to appeal to what his senses and especially his sight can assure him of, unwilling to walk by faith only. And he has an inbuilt wish to impose himself on others, to bend them to his will, and if possible to have some visible proof of his mastery over them. All these things belong to that inherent self-centredness that marks human existence and is described by Paul as 'flesh', when that word is used in its theological sense, as the opposite of love, which goes out to the neighbour, and the opposite of Spirit, or God-centred existence. It is Paul's ability to see this behind the work of the Judaizers that gives Galatians its permanent significance and value in the life of the Church. I asked whether Paul was being fair to the Judaizers; it is a natural question to ask but it may turn out in the end to be an irrelevant one, for, as far as immediate motivation goes, Paul's allegations can be taken in different ways. The way that lies on the surface supposes that he was referring to conscious motives of which the Judaizers, had they been prepared to admit it, must have been well aware. They said, 'We think you ought to obey God's plain command'; but they meant, 'We want to bend you to our will, we want to see in your flesh, in your physical bodies, the sign that we have triumphed over you, the sign that shows – for our benefit as well as your own – that you belong to our party.' It may be, however, that Paul was analysing submerged, unconscious motives, that he saw more clearly into what the Judaizers were doing than they saw themselves. He would say to them, 'You say, and maybe you think, that you are obediently insisting upon the importance of God's command; but truly you are seeking a substitute for grace, a substitute for faith, a substitute for obedience to God in obedience to yourselves.' It is this kind of submerged motivation, which calls not for psychological so much as theological analysis, that has again and again played havoc with Christian theology and Christian institutions, and again and again it has been right to say, 'You believe that you are speaking in the name of God and requiring only what he requires, but in fact you are despising grace, denying faith and seeking power over your brothers rather than serving them through love; you profess to be guided by the Spirit but you are glorying in the flesh.'

Secondly, they wish to avoid persecution for the cross of Christ. So (looking at this historically) there was persecution for the cross of Christ. Paul presumably knew this from both sides. He had himself persecuted the Church (1.13); and he had been, and still was, persecuted (5.11; cf. 4.29). We may reasonably infer that in each case the ground of the persecution was centred upon the cross. As we have seen, Deuteronomy 21.23 was probably used to prove that Jesus was under God's curse; his followers were thus perpetuating a curse within Judaism and must be persecuted out of it. Moreover, though Jesus was crucified by the Romans, he had been cast out by Judaism; the Sanhedrin had decided against him, probably regarding him as a blasphemer, a false prophet, who was leading Israel astray. He must therefore have been in error, and his crucifixion proved this. There are references elsewhere in the New Testament to the persecution of Christians by Jews, and there is no reason to think that it did not take place; the exclusion of Christians from the synagogue by means of the so-called Test Benediction (*birkath ham-minim*) was nearer to the end than the beginning of the process. There is also evidence for the persecution of Paul by Jewish Christians (2 Corinthians 11.26), and no doubt the Christians who took Paul's line would receive the same treatment. To require circumcision, however, in addition to acceptance of the gospel, would ease the pressure, even if the gospel was understood (as in 1 Corinthians 15.3) to include reference to the cross. Non-Christian Jews might say, 'These people are at least being brought by circumcision into the Jewish fold, even if they hold undesirable views about Jesus of Nazareth.' It seems to me that here too we may and must distinguish between consciously held motives and the theological analysis of unconsciously held motives. The Judaizers may have been courageous men who would willingly have faced persecution had they believed that this was required of them. Their conscious motive may have been one that Paul himself shared: to purify Judaism in terms of a true understanding of the word of God in the Old Testament, to do justice to the stock of God's olive tree (Romans 11.17–24), to recognize the immutability of his promise to the fathers (Romans 11.28, 29). But they were doing this through loyalty to an institution, a possibly persecuting institution, with which they had no intention of breaking.

Paul might with advantage have used a few more sentences here in order to make clear the theological analysis he was pursuing. He may however have seriously – and not impossibly wrongly – believed that the Judaizers were consciously motivated in the way he describes: they really did wish to have a secure life and to be thought persons of significance and authority. If so, they were neither the first nor the last. But it will be seen that we have been able to move out of history through ethics, and into theology; and it is for Paul's critical theology that we have to be most grateful.

I wrote earlier (pp. 57f.) of 'the circumcised' (οἱ περιτεμνόμενοι, present participle) in 6.13. I do not think we can see here a reference to Gentiles now having themselves circumcised. If I am right in this, Paul is accusing fellow Jews, 'the circumcised', of not keeping the law. How is this to be explained? There are several possibilities. One is to take this accusing clause closely with the adversative clause that follows: 'in demanding your circumcision they are not keeping the law but indulging a desire to glory in your flesh. It is not the law but their own sense of self-importance that impels them to act as they do.' A second possibility is that their observance of the law does not come up to the strict Pharisaic standards that Paul himself has observed in the past (Philippians 3.5; Galatians 1.14) and would presumably still regard as correct, if the law were to be observed at all. A third possibility is that they did not keep the law in the way in which it had been deepened and radicalized by Jesus, and by Paul himself; that is, they may have been circumcised, have observed the Sabbath, and maintained the dietary laws, but they did not love their neighbours. How concerned Paul continued to be about the old Pharisaic standards we do not know; had he meant to accuse his opponents of lack of love he would probably have said so. The first possibility is therefore the one we may prefer. It accords with Paul's critical theology of the law as we see it elsewhere: the law rightly understood in the light of Jesus does not require a circumcising mission.

Between verses 13, 14 there is a clear link in the word 'glory': they wish to glory in your flesh; I will glory in nothing but the cross of our Lord Jesus Christ. There is a more important theological link in the critical theology of which I have just spoken, for Paul's theology is, as we have seen, the theology of *solus Christus*, and its critical cutting edge is the cross. Nothing is more directly opposed to *flesh*, egocentric existence, than the cross of Christ. Egocentric existence means the desire to be served and to acquire; the Son of man 'came not to be served but to serve, and to give himself a ransom for many' (Mark 10.45). 'He loved me, and gave himself for me' (2.20). It is to this touchstone that every proposition in theology, every course of action prescribed in ethics, every Christian institution must be brought. There are some theologies, some courses of action, some institutions that are absolutely inconsistent with this standard; and even those theologies that are relatively correct, those actions that are relatively proper, those institutions that are relatively unobjectionable, constitute no ground for glorying. The whole of Paul's criticism of the Judaizing, circumcising movement crystallizes here; and it is the ground of self-criticism that the Church has to apply in every generation.

Verses 14b, 15 contain further material which is of vital importance if we are to understand Paul's theology of salvation. They contain respectively the two fundamental aspects of it.

Through the cross (or perhaps we should say, through Christ; in any case, through Christ crucified)[68] 'the world has been crucified to me and I to the world'. This states the existential, anthropological content or aspect of salvation in vivid terms. My existence consists in my relation to my environment, in the constant interaction between myself and the world of which I am part and in which I move. Existence is not static substance but movement, as I respond to stimuli I receive from others, and in turn exert influence upon them. This existence in its old form is radically changed as my relation to the world about me is changed. I am crucified to it and it is crucified to me; the old relation, and with it the old existence, is annihilated, like the physical life of Jesus on the cross. My very being is broken up, like his body, together with its passions and lusts (5.24); I have been crucified with Christ and I live no longer; a new principle of being, Christ himself, operates within me (2.19, 20). This corresponds to the existential, anthropological analysis of man's *malaise*, which I noticed at an earlier point in the epistle (pp. 39f.). In these circumstances, with this total reorientation of my existence, I must neither compel another nor allow myself to be compelled to be circumcised. Circumcision and uncircumcision are totally irrelevant – and it is of course the would-be circumcisers who are treating them as relevant, not those who, like Paul, resist their claims.

This inference leads to the next verse, which depicts the other side of salvation. Circumcision is nothing, uncircumcision is nothing; what matters is a new creation – a new cosmic act on the part of God. We have moved away from the subjective, existential view of salvation to an objective, metaphysical view, which corresponds to the objective analysis of man's *malaise*, described as due to the usurping of power by elements of the cosmos, who have taken under their control and perverted God's good world (and incidentally God's good law). Crucifixion and resurrection, and all that flows from them, are comparable only with the creation of the world. This is an act independent of man's existential response to it, but the indispensable condition of this response.

It is worthwhile to pause for a moment to note how admirably the existential aspect of Paul's understanding of salvation has been expounded by Bultmann,[69] and that he has almost completely removed the cosmic aspect by demythologizing it back into the existential. This is an attractive procedure, for few of us today can be really at home with cosmic elements, with principalities and powers. But since Paul was quite capable of doing the demythologizing when he wished we must suppose that, when he did not do it, but allowed the elements to stand, he did not intend to do it, but intended to leave room for an objective aspect. Whether we can express the objective element in his terms is a fair question, but whether we can do without it is another. There may be a pointer, which we cannot now follow up, in 2 Corinthians 5.15–17. There we see clearly how the world (cf. Galatians 6.14) is – myself; for parallel to 'the world has been crucified to me and I to the world' we have 'that they which live should no longer live to themselves', and the reference to new creation follows in the context of a new understanding of Christ and of men in general. We see once more, and perhaps now most clearly, that freedom is freedom to die with Christ by faith, and that it is inseparable from the obligation to live the life of love that Christ lives within the believer.

Thus Paul ends with a blessing upon the people of God, but he attaches to it a condition; the blessing applies to those who conform 'to this rule'. Has the law come back, after all? The word 'rule' is not the word for law. It is a measuring rod (κανών),[70] and it refers not to particular laws (unless perhaps to the summary law of love in 5.14), but to lives that are shaped by the gospel.

Verse 17 is not to be taken literally except in the sense that Paul bore branded on his body marks of suffering he had endured for Christ's sake, beatings, stonings, shipwreck and the like. This makes a paradox of the theme of marking, for, in Paul's world, such marks were on the one hand a sign of ownership – a runaway slave brought back to his owner might be branded to make it clear that he was not his own master but belonged to the man whose mark he bore, and on the other hand a sign of protection – the supernatural power invoked by the mark would protect his servant. Paul's sufferings were a clear enough mark of the fact that he belonged, body and soul, to Christ; paradoxically they meant too, not that Christ would see to it that he never suffered, but that Christ would never leave him to his fate: persecuted but not forsaken, cast down but not destroyed (2 Corinthians 4.9).

Throughout this letter Paul is writing theology, convinced, as I have said, that the practical problems of church life are theological problems and therefore need theological solutions. But the theology is Pauline theology, and that means that it is never abstract or remote; rooted as it is in the incarnate, suffering, dying Jesus it can never be that. It is not an academic theology, yet it is as profound as it is practical. The last verses of the letter make the application of the theology particularly clear.

It is historicized: for it is theology that lies behind the work of the Judaizers, just as it is a different theology that lies behind Paul's resistance to it. They would have given – and we need not doubt their sincerity, though Paul seems to have done so – a different account of their motives from that which appears in verses 12, 13; yet Paul's analysis was essentially right. The theology of *solus Christus* is wounding to man's pride, not least his religious pride, but it is the way of freedom.

The theology is ethicized: the freedom of faith is inextricably linked with the obligation of love, since each equally finds its origin in Christ.

The theology is individualized: this is written on every page up to the last. There was a special sense in which Paul bore in his own person the marks of Jesus, but it was not he alone who could confess his faith in 'the Son of God who loved me and gave himself for me'; and we may give the last words to Luther:

> Read with great vehemency these words, 'me', and 'for me',
> and so inwardly practise with thyself, that thou, with a sure
> faith, mayst conceive and print this 'me' in thy heart, and apply
> it unto thyself, not doubting but that thou art of the number
> of those to whom this 'me' belongeth: also that Christ hath not
> only loved Peter and Paul, and given himself for them, but that
> the same grace also which is comprehended in this 'me', as well
> pertaineth and cometh unto us, as unto them.

Freedom and obligation are reconciled in God, in whom both are one, so that the only way to have obligation without legalism is to begin, as Paul does, with theology.

Apostles in Council and in Conflict

It may help to hold this chapter together if I begin by describing the two points from which my thinking has begun. Whether the two lines of investigation will converge sufficiently to constitute a coherent and meaningful theme will appear only as we proceed. I shall be obliged to introduce both points with a greater amount of autobiography than I should wish.

The first is this. It has not infrequently been my duty to lecture on the Acts of the Apostles. In doing this one comes to Chapter 15 and the account of the so-called Apostolic Council. When I have reached this point I have indicated the central importance of the event in Luke's narrative; I have drawn attention to the main exegetical problems in the chapter, and discussed them; I have summarized the views of leading commentators and historians of primitive Christianity; and there I have stopped. Perhaps I caricature myself; but − and this is my first starting-point − I cannot avoid the conviction that the time has now come when I must begin to clarify my conclusions regarding both Luke's intentions as he incorporates this chapter in his book, and the historical events which perhaps we may trace behind his narrative. 'Apostles in Council', therefore.

The second point of departure also is to be found in a belated attempt to make up a serious deficiency in teaching. After many years of lecturing on the Theology of the New Testament I decided that I had better make up my mind exactly what that title meant. What is New Testament Theology, and how is it related to, and how does it differ from, other branches of theology? In the pursuit of this question I have repeatedly found myself confronted by the question of the canon, which, I suppose, means the double question, 'What constitutes the New Testament?' and, 'What is the New Testament, thus constituted?' Is our list of twenty-seven books too large or too small? That is, should we look for a canon within the canon? Or should we include in the canon the whole of early Christian literature? In what sense can the New Testament be normative for Christian theology? This leads to the present investigation. Suppose it to be true (and this is to be investigated) that behind the Council of Acts 15 there can be seen a division, a deep-seated disagreement in belief and practice, between those apostles whose authority may be said to constitute canonicity, what becomes of the canon? Hence, 'Apostles in conflict'.

It will be clear that a full treatment of either of these topics taken on its own would extend far beyond the scope of a single essay. The one is investigative and descriptive, the other theological, involving reflection upon biblical data. I hope not to fall between two stools, giving inadequate treatment to each topic, because it is precisely the relation between the two that constitutes my real theme. What I think we may hope to see is the way in which the issue of the Council first exacerbates the problem of the New Testament canon (and there is such a problem) and then provides if not a solution of the problem at least the possibility of looking at it in a fresh and constructive light.

So we begin with the historical problem of the Apostolic Council and the cross-currents of early Christian history that lie behind it. I do not think it necessary to take up the question whether, in Acts 15, Luke was dependent on written sources or wrote up in his own way such information as he had acquired orally. Dibelius and Haenchen may have seemed to decide the matter on the lines of the latter alternative, but Bultmann and Hengel (to name no others) have defended the probability of written sources. It seems to me perverse to deny either possibility. Luke would seek an account from anyone who might have one to give him; and there is no reason why some of the accounts should not have been on paper. And who could distinguish with confidence between Luke's writing up of the stories he was told by word of mouth and his editing of written material? What the work of past generations has shown beyond doubt is that Luke's narrative is patchy; it has been put together from more than one source, and though it contains material of historical value the history can be reconstructed only if we are prepared to take to pieces the story as it stands and examine the several parts of which it is composed. That there was a gathering in Jerusalem at which the relation of Gentiles to gospel and Church was discussed, and, to some extent, settled is proved by Galatians 2, though the exact relation between the two chapters is disputed. I shall not discuss it now but allow myself to say that the difficulties – and there are not a few – involved in taking Galatians 2 and Acts 15 to be roughly parallel to each other are far less than the difficulties involved in supposing that the recognition of a Gentile gospel reached at one gathering was so speedily forgotten that a year or two later the whole issue had to be thrashed out again with no reference to the earlier discussion and decision, or in the view that Galatians 2 should be related to Acts 18.

With these preliminary observations we may consider some points in the text of Acts 15.

What (according to Luke) was the debate about? It begins in Antioch when people come down from Jerusalem and say to Gentile converts, 'Unless you are circumcised in accordance with the custom of Moses, you cannot be saved' (15.1). This is taken up when, in verse 5, the scene is transferred to Jerusalem, for we must understand the necessity there referred to (δεῖ περιτέμνειν) as describing what is necessary for salvation. Those who make this demand are concerned with the way in which Christianity is to be presented to the hearer. If he asks (like the Philippian gaoler in Acts 16.30), 'What must I do to be saved?' the answer will doubtless include that which is given by Paul in that passage, but it will include also an essential supplement: 'Believe on the Lord Jesus Christ, be circumcised, observe the rest of the law of Moses, and you will be saved.' Salvation (except where σώζειν, σωτηρία, are used in a non-religious sense, 4.9; 7.25; 14.9; 27.20, 31, 34) regularly appears in Acts as the result of the Christian proclamation. The gospel message is the word of this salvation (13.26); the Christian preachers proclaim the way of salvation (16.17). Peter ends his speech on the Day of Pentecost with the appeal, 'Save yourselves from this perverse generation' (2.40), and claims that there is no salvation to be had except in Christ (4.12). The angel tells Cornelius that Peter will speak words by which he and his household will be saved (11.14). It is the Christian message that tells men how they are to be saved, and it may therefore be said that the controversialists whose polemical assertions set the narrative of Acts 15 in motion are concerned with Christian preaching, and insist that it must contain reference to the Mosaic requirements. The discussion then is to be about preaching, about the content of the gospel. It is worth while to note the parallel between this and the evidence of Galatians. When Paul went up to Jerusalem he submitted (ἀνεθέμην) to the authorities there 'the Gospel that I preach among the Gentiles' (2.2). He does not say that he sought accreditation for himself (though this was a related matter) or that he was asking for some special status or relationship for the churches he had founded. The theme of proclamation continues through the paragraph, and in fact provides the occasion for the writing of the epistle. The Galatians were turning to another gospel, which in fact was no gospel at all (1.6 f.).

Paul, then, and the narrative that Luke has constructed, begin with the theme of preaching, the question in what terms the Christian message is to be stated and presented to the world. How does the discussion proceed? Who were present, and what contributions did they make? Here too there is some real but limited correspondence between the two accounts. We have already seen that the narrative in Acts is set in motion by the arrival in Antioch of persons who came from Judaea and insisted on the circumcision of Gentile converts (15.1). Their position was taken up in Jerusalem by believing Pharisees (15.5); we can hardly distinguish between the two groups and it is unlikely that Luke did so. No doubt, in his view, they were Christian Pharisees who went to Antioch. He probably thinks also that they were responsible for the great argument of 15.7; at least, there is no sign in his story of any other divergent view, and they fell silent (15.12) at the end of Peter's speech. Are these Christian Jews to be identified with the 'false brothers' of Galatians 2.4? Paul's language is harsher, and he attributes to the false brothers underhand tactics – they had been smuggled in in order to act as spies – which do not appear in Acts. Moreover, it seems in Galatians that Paul takes on these opponents single-handed; there is no suggestion that Peter had a share in dealing with them. We hear nothing, in Acts 15 or in Galatians 2, of their side of the discussion. Neither Luke nor Paul (in Galatians 2) tells us by what arguments they supported their view of the Christian message of salvation. In fact, in Acts the Council takes on the appearance of a sham fight; the people were behind Paul (15.3, 4, cf. 31) and there was no serious opposition. This is already an indication of some inadequacy in Luke's account; Luke knows only one side of the debate.

In addition to the unnamed upholders of the requirement of circumcision Acts tells us of the participation of Peter, Paul, Barnabas and James. Galatians adds John. We must consider the speeches ascribed by Luke to these participants.

Peter introduces himself as the first preacher of the gospel to Gentiles. He was chosen by God for this purpose, and recalls that the response of his Gentile hearers was simply to believe. This, says Peter, is common knowledge, and it goes back to the earliest days of Christianity in Jerusalem. Peter of course is referring to his visit to the household of the centurion Cornelius, described at length in Acts 10 and recapitulated in Acts 11. This story was probably found by Luke in Caesarea where it was told as the origin of the mixed Jewish and Gentile church in the city. We must keep it in mind, for it contains twice over the same kind of problem that we shall meet when we come to the Decree which (according to Luke) was the outcome of the Council. Early in the story (10.10–16) Peter sees a vision of clean and unclean beasts; when bidden to slaughter for himself he declines on the ground that he has never eaten unclean food; he is then admonished, 'What God has cleansed do not you count unclean.' Later, however, when referring to the vision, he says that God has taught him to consider no *man* (μηδένα ἄνθρωπον, emphatic; 10.28) unclean. In Acts 11 this movement of thought is reversed. Those who object to Peter's action complain at first that he has eaten with uncircumcised men (11.3), but at the end of his report agree that it has been shown that God has granted to the Gentiles also the repentance that leads to life (11.18); that is, in the language of 15.1, they may as Gentiles be saved. This story Peter recalls in 15.7–9, stressing the fact that God acted in relation to the Gentiles on the basis of faith, without legal requirement (πίστει in verse 9 as well as πιστεῦσαι in verse 7). The conclusion of his speech in verses 10, 11 is expressed in a rhetorical question which introduces a new argument. To impose the law upon Gentile converts to Christianity would lay upon them a burden that 'neither we nor our fathers were able to bear'. Conzelmann rightly remarks that this is not the Jewish attitude to the law which, though it might be described as a yoke, is a yoke which it is a privilege and a joy to wear – certainly not an intolerable load. This is how the law appeared to the rabbis, including the rabbi Saul of Tarsus (Philippians 3.4–7). Perhaps it was different for a Galilean '*am ha'areṣ*. This is a serious possibility; the unsatisfactory attitude of the Galileans to Torah has been emphasized of late. But there are difficulties here. Even in Galilee circumcision was no problem; a child eight days old had little opportunity to complain at the time and no occasion to do so subsequently. As for food laws, we have Peter's word in Acts 10.14 that he had never touched unclean food. This is indeed a problem. Whatever his habits as an '*am ha'areṣ* may have been, had he learned nothing from Jesus? We must, it seems, choose between Peter the strict observant of the law (Acts 10) and Peter who finds the law an intolerable burden (Acts 15) on this point, but even if we choose the latter our difficulties are not at an end, for the reference to 'our fathers' is not only dangerously comprehensive, it suggests a reference to tradition, and Jewish tradition was certainly on the side of food laws and other legal requirements, which it regarded not as a burden but as a privilege.

The words attributed to Peter were almost certainly composed by Luke, who in writing the speech had a difficult task. In his day, as is clearly shown by 1 Peter and 1 Clement, Peter had the reputation of being one of great pioneer missionaries, who operated in parallel with Paul. He certainly had relations with Gentiles, as is proved by the old Caesarean tradition of Acts 10 and by Galatians 2.12 (he used to eat with the Gentiles). The tradition about Jesus (as Luke himself records it) connected Peter closely with him. So Luke represents him as the first missionary to the Gentiles, as the representative of the original disciples of Jesus who could be expected accurately to transmit the Master's mind on disputed matters, and as the exponent of Pauline theology. It is in the last of these points that Luke is least successful. The emphasis on faith is Pauline enough, but when in verse 11 grace and salvation are added the result is an un-Pauline confusion; and none knew better than Paul how attractive the law could be to mankind.

In verse 12 Barnabas and Paul take their turn. All that Luke has to say about them is that they recounted the signs and portents that God had done through them among the Gentiles. Haenchen remarks[71] that Luke, lacking Paul's critical theological understanding of the law, is obliged to justify the Gentile mission by miracles. This is hardly fair to Luke, who has put into the debate a number of arguments – Peter's pragmatic argument (no doubt Luke's own), that Gentiles in fact manifest the same spiritual gifts as Jews, and Peter's supposedly Pauline argument (also Luke's own), that the law has always been an intolerable burden; the argument attributed to Barnabas and Paul, that miracles prove God's approval, and therefore the validity of the mission; and James's argument, that Scripture gives a prophetic forecast of God's intention to take a people for himself out of the Gentiles. This is a many-stranded proof, capable of serious theological exposition – which, in Acts, it does not receive. It is however paradoxical that the argument based on miracles should be assigned to Paul, who, though he does twice (Romans 15.19; 2 Corinthians 12.12) refer to the signs that accompanied his ministry, does not use them as validation of his work. It is hard to believe that he made this his one contribution to the debate.

With this observation we may put another. In both accounts of the Council there are notable absentees. As we have seen, Paul mentions, in addition to the false brothers, himself and Barnabas (Titus serves rather as a test case or provocation than as a participant), with James, Cephas and John. Luke mentions, in addition to apostles and elders (15.6; the πλῆθος of verse 12 and the ἐκκλησία of verse 22 do not imply active participation by the rank and file of the Jerusalem church), Peter, Barnabas, Paul and James. Neither of our authorities mentions the Hellenists. From Paul's account we may infer the simple explanation: they are not mentioned because they were not there. This accords with Acts 8.1: they had been driven from Jerusalem. But this verse, though it occurs in his own book, is hardly a sufficient reason for Luke's omission of the Hellenists from his account of the Council. Stephen has made a slashing attack on Jewish institutionalism (Acts 7). Philip, not Peter, is in the strict sense the first preacher to Gentiles; he preaches to the Samaritans and his converts include Simon Magus, who was not an orthodox Samaritan, let alone a Jew; he preaches the good news of Jesus to the Ethiopian eunuch and baptizes him, though this convert can have been no more than a godfearer, as apparently Cornelius was. They are Hellenists, scattered by the persecution that arose over Stephen (11.19), who preach in Antioch, at first to Jews only, but then also to Greeks (i.e. Gentiles, 11.20). On the basis of Luke's own story they had as good a right as anyone to be represented at the Council; why were they not? The historical answer may well be, They were not there because they were no longer in Jerusalem and could not be summoned. Luke's answer seems to be, They were there, represented by Paul and Barnabas. This answer is carefully prepared for and supported. Paul is brought into the story of Stephen's martyrdom (7.58; 8.1), and his work as a persecutor is connected with it (8.3); it is on a persecuting trip to Damascus that his conversion takes place (9.1–3). At Acts 22.20 Paul recalls his presence when Stephen's blood was shed, and it seems clear that Luke, rightly or wrongly, attributed to the martyrdom a psychological effect leading to the conversion. This is backed up by the participation of Barnabas and Paul in the founding, by Hellenists, of the church in Antioch (11.19, 22, 25f.). The two are named among the ministers of the church there (13.1–3) and are sent out as missionaries commissioned by it (13.3). At the end of the 'first missionary journey' they return to report to the church that had sent them out (14.26–8). It is at Antioch that the dispute leading to the Council arises (15.1; 15.2, 3, in the non-Western text, suggest but do not quite prove that Barnabas and Paul were sent to Jerusalem to represent Antioch). The inference is clear. In the Acts Council Barnabas and Paul represent the Hellenists because they share in and continue the work of Stephen and other Hellenists (including Philip; cf. 21.8). There are further inferences, of considerable importance. Along with Peter, the second main strand of Christian life and preaching contributes to the discussion and its eventual result. This is Luke's intention, but he has shown himself unable to distinguish two lines of preaching, two ways of setting out the message of Jesus, that were in fact distinct. He has assimilated Paul and Peter, now Paul and the Hellenists. He deals with the divisions of the early Church by denying that they exist, or rather, by failing to understand that there were significant differences in the way the different groups apprehended and presented the Gospel.

We turn next to James's contribution. The greater part of this is made up of a quotation from Amos 9.11f., though it has rightly been pointed out by Dupont that the Old Testament allusions begin in 15.14. These allusions however reveal misunderstanding of the Old Testament passages, which speak of God's action in choosing Israel out of all the nations to be his own peculiar people. The words are taken by James (as his reference to Peter – Symeon – shows) to refer not to God's election of Israel but to his adding of Gentiles to his original Jewish people. This misinterpretation prepares us for James's use of Amos, where by following the LXX he is able to elicit a meaning almost opposite to that of the Hebrew. The facts have often been noted and can be found in any commentary; we hear nothing of the possessing of Edom by Israel, but that the rest of men, that is, men other than Israel, all the Gentiles, will seek the Lord, and presumably, since this is the declared will of God, will find him. Is it possible that James, about whom we have other information, should, in a Jerusalem conference, have used the Greek text of the Old Testament when this comes near to contradicting the Hebrew? Notwithstanding Gerhardsson's arguments to the contrary, it seems most unlikely that he would do so. It is true that rabbis would use any text they could find if it would support the interpretation they wished to give. But in such cases the Massoretic text usually appears as a base and the preferred reading is given as an alternative, for example in the *'al tiqre'* formula: 'Do not read X, but Y' (p. 45). There is no trace of this in Acts 15. It may be that Luke did not perceive, or did not understand, James's method, and cut his corners in reaching the desired result, but this also would result in a misinterpretation of James.

Of verse 20, which anticipates the contents of the Decree, I shall say nothing at this point, but it is worth while to glance at verse 21. The place of this verse in the logic of the developing argument is disputed and I shall not discuss it at length. We may however note the claim that Moses is regularly read in the synagogues and has those who proclaim him. There is no need therefore to preach Moses; he has preachers enough. James is agreeing that in the new proclamation it is the new Christian element that is the concern of the apostles; Moses is already well represented. Verse 21 probably contains within it the two strands that appear in verses 19, 20: 'It is not necessary to trouble them, but...' So here: we do not need to preach Moses, but we must bear in mind the fact that there are those who do. The theme of proclamation continues.

This observation provides the cue for the point I wish to make. Luke is aware that an important conference on the position of Gentiles in relation to the Christian gospel took place. In this awareness he is quite correct; that there was such a conference is amply confirmed by Galatians. He is also correct in seeing that the question turned on the nature of the proclamation, and in this too he is confirmed by Galatians. In Galatians 2.5 Paul takes the stand that he does 'in order that the truth of the gospel might continue with you'. In verse 7 he claims to have been entrusted with the gospel. In verse 9 it is agreed that 'we should go to the Gentiles, they to the circumcision' – evidently with a view to preaching to them. There are matters here to which we must return; for the present we note simply that the conference is about preaching, the instrument used by God for salvation.

So far Luke is right; but only so far. He has failed to differentiate the different kinds of preaching and has thereby made something like nonsense of the debate – for it is a curious debate (a sham fight, I said earlier), in which every one agrees with everyone else. In fact we may distinguish no fewer than five lines of preaching, of gospel, in the New Testament; that they are distinguishable does not mean that they were contradictory, or that only one of them was legitimate. Galatians makes it clear that there was a gospel of the circumcision, entrusted to Peter, and that this was not the same thing as the gospel of the uncircumcision that was entrusted to Paul. The fact that these were not identical is confirmed by 1 Corinthians; had they been identical we should not have had some who said 'I am of Cephas', others 'I am of Paul'. There is, in addition, weight in F. C. Baur's argument that the superficial agreement apparently reached in Galatians 2 must have contained a hypocritical element (pp. 12, 60). If the 'pillars' had truly agreed with Paul and his gospel they would have joined him in preaching it to the Gentile world, as in fact they did not. This is certainly true of James; not so true of Peter, who is found in the Gentile world. The position of Peter is difficult, perhaps impossible, to define precisely because, it seems, it lacked stability (Galatians 2.12f., ὑπόκρισις). Paul, and probably James too, knew his own mind and adhered to principles of action; Peter was drawn this way and that by well-intentioned impulses, and lacked the power to assess critically suggestions that were put to him. We may speak of a distinctive Petrine Gospel only with this important qualification.

Galatians 2.12 is sufficient to show that James took a line that was different from Paul's, different also from Peter's, when Peter was left to his own devices, or was under the influence of Paul. It is however important to see where James's position differed from Paul's. It did not differ in that he demanded the circumcision of Gentile converts to Christianity (so that we may note at once that he is not to be classed with the false brothers who did demand complete loyalty to the customs of Moses, including circumcision). He was prepared to allow the existence of a gospel of the uncircumcision; but he insisted with a consistency not found in Peter that there should be a corresponding but different gospel of the circumcision, according to which Jews who accepted the Messiahship of Jesus, and the belief that in him the messianic salvation had become available, must continue to be in every sense Jews. This of course led to the necessary conclusion that they must not eat with Christians of Gentile origin unless these became not only Christians but also Jews by proselytization.

In addition to these groups headed by Paul, Peter and James, there were the false brothers, whose message was 'Believe in Jesus as Messiah and accept the law'; and the Hellenists. In one sense, these last are the most shadowy figures of all, chiefly because, as we have seen, Luke seems to regard them as adequately represented by Paul and Barnabas, whereas in fact they were not present and not represented. There is however one point in the Acts account where we may see their hand at work. This is in the Decree which emerges (15.29) as the result of the Council.

It is fairly widely agreed that though, as I have argued in this chapter, the speeches attributed to Peter and James, and those hinted at for Paul and Barnabas, are Luke's own work, the Decree itself is traditional material, just as the fact of the Council was. It is there because Luke found it in operation in some, perhaps most, of the churches of his own day, and not unnaturally connected it with the Council of which he had also heard. In this he was mistaken, for it is clear that Paul either had never heard of the Decree, or chose, if he had heard of it, to ignore it. This is as certain as any negative conclusion may be. He exhorts his readers to flee from fornication (1 Corinthians 6.18), but does not mention the Decree, to flee from idolatry (1 Corinthians 10.14), but does not mention the Decree; and, in flat contradiction of the Decree, he tells them that they may buy any food offered for sale in the public market, and eat any food set before them by a heathen host (1 Corinthians 10.25, 27). The Decree then is not Paul's work, nor is it the work of out-and-out Judaizers, who would not be satisfied with anything less then circumcision and the whole law. A good case can be made for dating the Decree not at the Council but after it, at the time of the controversy in Antioch recorded in Galatians 2.11f. Whatever the various parties concerned had understood by the agreement reached at the Council, they had not envisaged the life of a mixed, partly Jewish, partly Gentile, church, such as that at Antioch, in which Jews and Gentiles, all of them Christians, joined in common meals. Paul, and at first Peter and Barnabas, shared this practice, the first of them regarding it as a necessary consequence of the gospel he preached. When word of this reached James he sent a message pointing out that such indiscriminate eating with Gentiles meant that Jews were ceasing to be Jews; they were no longer observing the law, and the admission of Gentiles without circumcision was never intended (that is, by him) to carry with it the de-Judaizing of Jews. Jews were therefore bidden to withdraw from communion with Gentile Christians. The resulting position was clearly an impossible one. Two parties dug in their heels and refused to budge. One was Paul, who publicly rebuked Peter as a hypocrite and would have no compromises. Gentile Christians were Christians, members of the one people of God, who with their Jewish brethren ate one loaf and one loaf only. The other party was that of the Judaizers, the false brothers, false apostles, preachers of a different gospel which (according to Paul) was not a gospel at all. Galatians itself is sufficient to prove their continuing existence and continuing demand for the circumcision of all Gentile converts. Others were prepared to compromise. Peter, when people came from James, withdrew and separated himself – out of fear, says Paul. So did the other Jewish Christians, including even Barnabas. Yet these men had previously acted differently, and, especially if it be true that they acted now out of fear, cannot simply have changed their convictions. It is the very fact that Peter was acting contrary to his true convictions that so angers Paul. They had been forced into a position with which they could not be content. This was a situation for compromise.

I suggest that the Decree was in fact the Hellenist compromise. Barnabas had thrown in his lot with the Antiochene church, which originated in Hellenist enterprise. Peter, if we are to think of him as a Galilean *'am ha'areş*, was on the way to Hellenism, and his contact with Jesus will have pushed him further in that direction. From this point, it seems, Barnabas separated from Paul (though Paul could still think of him as a sort of colleague, 1 Corinthians 9.6); and Peter appears as a rival authority (though Paul never refers to him as an enemy, cf. 1 Corinthians 3.22; 9.5). That the Decree was Hellenist in origin is well-nigh proved by its widespread use in the Gentile churches of the post-apostolic period, for these were Hellenist rather than Pauline. Luke probably found it operating in Antioch; hence his essentially correct though confused perception that the controversy behind the Council originated in Antioch (15.1) and was resolved when the Decree was received there (15.30f.). The Hellenists were Jews, however liberal; they appear in Jerusalem according to Acts 6.1 but they had roots in the Greek world. This (if we can make anything of Stephen's speech in Acts 7) may well have resulted in depreciation of the Temple ('We can maintain our religion without it', the Hellenists argued, 'we have to'), but at the same time an insistence on precisely those features of Judaism that are found in the Decree: worship of the one God, with no participation in idolatry; fundamental morality ('We must keep out of the Greek brothels – that has always been the way into heathenism'), and basic food laws. The one characteristic insistence of Diaspora Judaism that is missing is the observance of the Sabbath; the day of the resurrection, the first day of the week, had taken over from the seventh. James himself had, according to the old tradition (1 Corinthians 15.7), been a witness of the risen Christ. The preaching of the resurrection united all Christians (1 Corinthians 15.11).

The question that is now left unanswered is whether James accepted this compromise. Did it seem good to him to eat with Gentiles who were observing the terms of the Decree and thus accept the unity of circumcised and uncircumcised Christians in one body? One can reply only that we do not know. We do know that the Judaizers kept up their contact with some sort of base in Jerusalem. We have some reason to think that James had with non-Christian Jews a reputation for Jewish piety. It may well be that he was in the fortunate position of not having to make up his mind. The Hellenists had left Jerusalem, and James cannot often have had to decide whether or not he should eat with Gentile Christians.

So much for the historical, investigative part of this essay. What may we learn from it?

One point may be dealt with quickly. The New Testament contains, in Acts and Galatians, two accounts of one event; and these accounts are by no means identical. It is only the strict fundamentalist who will find a problem here, though it is to be hoped that he will find one and that he will think about it. There are many examples of such disagreements in the Bible. The three accounts in Acts of the conversion of Paul are ready to hand, and as everyone knows John does not date the crucifixion on the same day as the Synoptic Gospels. Once the notion is given up that the New Testament is, or claims to be, an infallible source of historical information there is no difficulty in such disagreements. The word of God clothes itself in the words of men, and no man is an infallible historian. The matter is familiar and need not be discussed further but it will be well to make a note of one conclusion: there is at least one thing that 'canon' does not mean. It does not mean an infallible account of historical events. If it must mean this, we have no canonical literature. Evident enough, though the contrary was long believed. Perhaps, notwithstanding traditional opinions, there are other things with which canon has as little to do.

The real problem as it touches the canon is twofold. In the first place, it appears not only from the story of the Apostolic Council but from the evidence of the New Testament at large that there were not only different styles of preaching (as for example those of Paul and Apollos) but also different proclamations, different ways of understanding what the Christian message is. In a famous essay Käsemann asked the question, 'Does the New Testament canon establish the unity of the Church?' A related question is whether the New Testament contains a single gospel or several varieties of gospel. We may have to ask whether the variety of gospels destroys the notion of a canon. In the second place there is the fact that the variety of proclamation is glossed over in the narrative of Acts 15, in which Barnabas and Paul (who evidently were not entirely at one between themselves) are made to serve as representative Hellenists, which they were not, Peter is made to speak as if he were Paul, and James to agree with all three. The variety of gospels is veiled in the interests of Christian unity; or, to put the matter more fairly, it is veiled because when Luke wrote it no longer existed in the old form, which had been forgotten and no longer had any reality for Luke and his contemporaries who all lived in a Church which had come to be united on Hellenist lines – the lines to which all participants in the debate adhere. If there was now a divergent form of preaching it was gnostic.

If we are to tackle this twofold problem we must begin from the observation that Luke and Paul are agreed at least in this, that the theme of the conference was preaching: 'What is the gospel the Church must preach?' Preaching is both a Lucan and a Pauline theme, though the two authors handle it in different ways. One of Luke's purposes in writing was to provide the preachers of his own day with examples on which they could base their own proclamation. In doing so, he distinguished between models determined not by their authors but by the audiences to which the sermons were addressed. We may speak of the sermons in the early chapters as Petrine, but this is the wrong designation. They are sermons addressed to Jews, synagogue sermons, and when Paul preaches in the synagogue at Pisidian Antioch he might almost as well be Peter. When he addresses a Greek audience at Athens, he speaks like a Hellenistic Jew, and not like the author of Romans 1; when he addresses the Ephesian elders at Miletus he does so in a style reminiscent of the way in which he writes to his churches. Variety is determined for Luke not by speaker but by audience.

Paul deals with the theme in a different way. Different preachers have different gospels and not all of them can be approved. There is no plainer statement of this than Galatians 1.6f.: the Galatians are falling away to a different gospel which is in fact not a gospel. Almost the same words occur in 2 Corinthians 11.4: the visitor to Corinth has brought with him a different gospel 'which you did not receive'. Yet this gospel undoubtedly is, or purports to be, a Christian message, since it involves Jesus and the Spirit, though according to Paul these are another Jesus and a different Spirit. These very passages however bear the implication that there might be a different gospel which truly is gospel; not identical with Paul's, but not for that reason to be totally disqualified. We recall the preachers of Philippians 1.14–18. Some speak the word of God out of envy and strife; they preach out of rivalry, with no pure intention, and with the appalling motive of 'adding affliction to my bonds'. One expects Paul to be hurt and angry; but he rejoices, because these preachers are preaching Christ.

There is truth on each side, Luke's and Paul's. Indeed Paul also distinguishes between gospels differing according to the audience to which they are addressed in Galatians 2.7, for it is hard to see in the gospel of the uncircumcision and the gospel of the circumcision anything but forms of the one gospel (that which Paul received as the instrument of salvation – 1 Corinthians 15.3) designed for commendation to Gentiles and Jews respectively. This is confirmed by the agreement of 2.9: 'We were to go to the Gentiles, they to the circumcision.' The gospel of the uncircumcision, which Paul preached to the Gentiles, can be to some extent reconstructed from his letters. It certainly did not require circumcision. Peter's gospel of the circumcision cannot be reconstructed in the same way, not only because we lack evidence, but also because, as we have seen, Peter had no firm theological base and was apt to adopt the colour of his environment. James was a more definite character, and if we compare his gospel with Paul's it is probably correct to say with F. C. Baur,[72] 'In the one [ἀποστολή] the Mosaic law is in force, in the other it is not', in the sense that James expected Christian Jews to continue to observe the law, whereas Paul permitted them to do so in some circumstances (1 Corinthians 7.18; cf. 9.20, 22), but not if such observance had the effect of throwing them out of communion with the Gentile church. Paul accepted so much divergence; yet it could only lead, and did lead, to further conflict.

In this sense, and in spite of Acts, we must recognize that the conference was a failure. Apostles in council became apostles in conflict. Yet the council was not wholly a failure. It recognized the central importance of establishing the message of salvation as the foundation of all Christian existence, and the principle that not every 'different gospel' was necessarily a false gospel; and it did something to establish limits within which this might be true. There are a number of hints which tell us fairly clearly what these limits were, or at least what Paul understood them to be. Certain people placed themselves outside the pale. Such were the Judaeans of Acts 15.1 and the false brothers of Galatians 2.4, whose interest in spying out 'our liberty which we have in Christ Jesus' was certainly practical rather than intellectual; they wished to put an end to it. The false apostles, the servants of Satan of 2 Corinthians

11.13–15 come under equal condemnation, and 11.3 suggests that they too had a radical supplement to make to simple faith directed towards Christ. It was the addition of law-based supplements, indeed the addition of any supplement to Christ crucified (1 Corinthians 2.2), that constituted the offence in Paul's eyes; this appears also from those passages that deal more positively with the question. We may recall those who sought by their preaching to add to Paul's sufferings but receive in Philippians a surprising welcome. They may have been malicious, but they preached Christ; there is no hint that they preached Christ and the law, as those who are attacked in Philippians 3.2f., 18f. apparently did. Most important of all, perhaps, is 1 Corinthians 15.1–11, taken in the context of the epistle as a whole. In agreement with his predecessors and contemporaries, with Cephas, James and all the apostles, Paul preaches the gospel by which men are saved, the gospel of Jesus, crucified and risen; and out of this gospel, without legalistic supplements, he evolves guidance for the ethical life of Christians. In this we may once more contrast Paul with Luke. Paul's story of the Council, which, historically, we must regard as primary, ends with an agreement – unsatisfactory, it is true – on the preaching of the Christian message. Paul will take his version of the gospel to the Gentiles, Peter will take his to the Jews. Acts 15 begins where Galatians 2 begins, but it ends with Clause 1 of the new Christian *Corpus Juris*.

The outcome of this long perambulation round perhaps too many mulberry bushes is clear. The apostolic Church, provoked by Paul, apart from whom it might not have acted, was concerned about the gospel; not its dogmatic formulation but the way in which it was to be presented to the non-Christian world, whether Jewish or Gentile. Before New Testament Scripture (in the strict sense of the term) existed, the New Testament Church, as attested in different ways by both Paul and Luke, took thought about a canon for preaching. H. Braun has referred to 'those writings in whose composition there was as yet no thought of canonization' as forming the heart of the New Testament canon.[73] He might have described the writings he has in mind as those which laid down no rigid rules for the systematic development of doctrine but manifested a profound concern for the purity of the preached word.

May we not on the basis of this observation consider further the nature of canonical Scripture, or rather of the doctrine of canonicity? What purpose is the canon of Scripture intended to serve?

As far as we know its earliest use was in relation to the reading of Scripture in church. In a famous passage (1 *Apology* 67) Justin writes: 'The memoirs of the apostles or the writings of the prophets are read as long as there is time. Then, when the reader has ceased, the president by his discourse give an admonition and exhortation to the imitation of these good things.' It is not said that the president preaches *on* the apostolic or prophetic works in the modern style, but his discourse is clearly related to and in harmony with them. A little later in the second century the Muratorian canon expresses its rejection of the *Shepherd* of Hermas thus: 'It is right that it should be read, but it cannot be read publicly (*publicare*) in church to the people to the end of time, either among the prophets, since their number is complete, or among the apostles.' A little earlier the same document reads: 'We receive only the Apocalypses of John and of Peter, which latter some of our people will not have read in church.' The language is not without obscurity, but it is clear that the canon is drawing a distinction between private reading and reading in church, which it is natural to connect with preaching. Westcott thought that *publicare* represented δημοσιεύεσθαι, and this word was used later of the reading of canonical works in church. So far as it means the publication of a matter to the δῆμος it is not far removed from preaching.

The intimate relation between the canon and preaching is no new discovery; as W. G. Kümmel remarks,[74] it was clearly recognized by Luther: 'Luther recognized that the books of the New Testament are in the full sense canonical in so far as they make the testimony to God's saving action in Christ audible in such a way that it can be further proclaimed.' According to Boehmer the connection runs back to Luther's understanding of the Word of God – far too complex a concept to be discussed by me, or in this setting: 'The Word of God is for Luther much more important than the sacraments, and the preaching of the Word of God, not the administration of the sacraments, is the chief task of the Church, for the Word is the means by which Christ founded the Church and maintains and governs it.'[75] We come even nearer to the point with a quotation from K. Holl:[76]

At the very time at which he composed the Prefaces [to the books of the Bible] Luther began to lay weight on the fact that the Gospel was in essence not a book, something composed in letters, but an 'oral preaching and a living word', 'a piece of good news and a shouted message', which has . . . sounded forth in all the world. That anything was ever written down at all is an expedient, an 'injury and damage', to the Spirit, caused by the misrepresentations to which the preaching was already exposed in the first generation.

It seems to me that we can derive from these observations conclusions that could be of considerable value. There could result a loosening up of the idea of canon, which has too often been seen in the light of a quarry from which could be dug out the trust-worthy building blocks out of which could be built the structures of church institutions and church dogmatics. The process can be seen already in Acts, where the Council which begins with a consideration of gospel preaching ends with the Decree. Paul's account does not, nor does Paul omit the explosion that accompanied the early piece of face-saving compromise which Luke found in the tradition that he used. This is not an attempt to stifle speculative theology, which can sometimes lead to truth, or the development of ecclesiastical institutions, which are necessary. The theologian, as Origen taught, must be free to go his own way, provided that he builds on Scripture and the rule of faith, and the church politicians will doubtless go theirs, whatever we say.

We may see also however, if we look from a different angle, a further truth, which will illuminate the relation between New Testament Theology and dogmatics. Each contributes to, and indeed is an aspect of, the primary task, which takes precedence of both, namely preaching. As Barth pointed out,[77] 'Preaching, if good preaching, is also exposition, and so is instruction, if it is good instruction. If it were not, it would be bad instruction. The Church's special science of dogmatics is also exposition. If it is not, it is bad dogmatics.' Dogmatics has been defined as the science by which the Church controls its preaching, and I have used this definition myself. But it might almost be reversed: true preaching becomes the criterion by which dogmatics must be judged and controlled. This however would oversimplify the relation between the two. All preaching contains a dogmatic element; dogmatics is a form of preaching. The canon therefore regulates primarily preaching; dogmatics, where it is practised, is a special-ized development of preaching. New Testament Theology contains within itself the elements of both preaching and dog-matics, and can be described as the critical process by which the canon controls both.

Notes

1   Betz, H. D., *Galatians* (Hermeneia Series) (Philadelphia 1979), p. xv. I shall refer several times to this excellent and up-to-date commentary, which is worthy to be set beside Lightfoot's classic work (London 1865, and many subsequent editions). Luther expounded Galatians more than once. I have quoted the translation of his later commentary published, with an introduction by E. Middleton, in 1860.

2   *Von der Freyheyt eines Christenmenschen.* 1520. The translation is that of H. Wace and C. A. Buchheim, *First Principles of the Reformation* (London 1883), p. 104.

3   Barth, K., *Church Dogmatics* I 1 ET (Edinburgh 1936), p. xiv.

4   In the 3rd century BC a number of Gallic tribes invaded Asia Minor and set up a Galatian kingdom in the north central part of what is now Turkey. It was a rural rather than an urban state, but had a few centres such as Ancyra, Pessinus, Tavium. The kingdom persisted till 25 BC, when its last king, Amyntas, bequeathed it to Rome. It became a province, but in the process a considerable tract of land to the south was added to it, so that the province extended almost to the south coast of Asia Minor. Books on Galatians and on Acts frequently refer to the originally Galatian territory as North Galatia, to the added territory as South Galatia, but it should be clearly understood that these terms, though possibly convenient, may be seriously misleading, since they were not used in antiquity. There is no evidence that the province was called Galatia in Paul's day, though later the term came into use. There is thus an *a priori* probability that for Paul the word Galatia would suggest the ancient kingdom. The additional, southern, territory was the scene of part of Paul's 'first missionary journey' (Acts 13.51—14.21: Iconium, Lystra, Derbe). If we accept the chronology of Acts we may say that he could have written to Galatia in this sense at any later point (Galatians 4.13 does not necessarily imply two visits). There is no account in Acts of missionary work in the northern territory, but (though this is disputed) Paul's presence in the territory is fairly clearly implied by Acts 16.6 (cf. 18.23). The southern territory had been covered in 16.1–5; 16.6 breaks fresh ground. Again, if we accept the chronology of Acts, Paul cannot have written to the northern territory till some point after Acts 16.6. Thus the geography of the epistle turns to some extent on its chronology, and vice versa. The main question here is that of Paul's visits to Jerusalem;

see notes 8 and 11. The use of 'Galatia', and especially the use of 'Galatians' (3.1), are in themselves strongly in favour of a northern destination.

5   For the view that Romans 7.7–25 is not to be taken as the record of a conversion experience I may refer to my commentary on Romans (London 1957), pp. 138–153; and to the same work, pp. 7–9, for the effect on Paul's understanding of law and eschatology of his discovery that Jesus was alive.

6   I have discussed this point in *The Signs of an Apostle* (London 1970), and in *New Testament Essays* (London 1972), pp. 80–2; I shall no doubt return to it in a forthcoming commentary on Acts. It is certainly true that Luke regards the apostles as important persons; equally certain that for him Paul was the outstanding missionary and leader of the first Christian generation. Yet only at Acts 14.4, 14 does he describe Paul as an apostle; at 14.14 the reading is in doubt (D gig h sy^p omit the word 'apostles') and at 14.4 it could be maintained that the meaning is, 'Some accepted the Jewish, others the apostolic, that is, the Christian, point of view.' In both verses the word 'apostle' (if read) is in the plural; that is, on the most natural reading of the familiar text, Barnabas also is an apostle. Luke's problem seems to have arisen primarily out of a rather wooden application of two principles: (a) there were twelve apostles, no fewer (so that Matthias must fill the place of the defecting Judas) and no more (so that there is no room for Paul); (b) an apostle must have been a companion of Jesus during his earthly ministry (Acts 1.21f.) – again Paul is disqualified. But it is probable that Acts reflects also both different uses of the word apostle and disputes about Paul's status. Such disputes are clearly visible in the epistles (e.g. 1 Cor. 9.2; 15.8f.) and form an important part of the background of Galatians. Paul emphasizes both his apostleship and his lack of the kind of authorization some would desiderate at 1.1. He shows how he understood his calling at 1.16, and at 1.17; 2.7 implies his claim to equality with others. At 2.8 it may not be insignificant that the word ἀποστολή, apostleship, is not repeated; did Jerusalem recognize Paul as an evangelist but not as an apostle? The epistle makes it clear that, in Paul's view, the validity of an apostolic ministry is demonstrated only by the truth of the gospel it proclaims.

7   There are important parallels between Galatians 1.15 and passages in the prophets, especially Jeremiah 1.5 (cf. Isaiah 44.2; 49.1, 6). This does not mean that we must describe what happened to Paul not as a conversion but a call. If the transformation of a persecutor into a preacher of the faith he formerly persecuted is not a conversion, a radical turning round so as to adopt a course opposite to that previously followed, I do not know where one is to be found. What

must be added is that every true conversion carries with it a call.

8   At 1.18, Paul says, 'Then after three years I went up to Jerusalem'; at 2.1, 'Then, after the space of fourteen years I went up again to Jerusalem.' It is not clear where the fourteen years interval begins; that is, whether or not the three years are included in it. Do we have to add the two intervals or not? Further, it was customary in antiquity to count inclusively, so that three years (part of one, a whole year, and part of another) might mean two years, or even little more than one. It might be safe to reckon 'three years' as twenty-four months, 'fourteen years' as 156 months. Thus an addition of the two periods might not add up to more than about fifteen years, though it might be a full seventeen.

9   The context (see the use of the verb ἀποκαλύψαι in v. 16) shows that what is meant is a disclosure of the risen Jesus, not an 'apocalypse given by Jesus Christ'.

10 I have deliberately written an ambiguous sentence because it is uncertain whether the Greek does or does not imply that James was an apostle. Paul was readier than some to use the word 'apostle' in a wide sense, and was probably prepared to believe that James was as much an apostle as Peter and John.

11 It seems that we do in fact have to choose between Galatians and Acts. Unless we can convince ourselves that the visit of Galatians 2 corresponds with that of Acts 11, 12, we have two visits over against three. Other solutions of the problem have been proposed (see especially Jewett, R., *Dating Paul's Life*. London 1979), but none seems to me so probable as that Luke has misunderstood two descriptions of one visit as accounts of two visits. Paul's own narrative in Galatians 2 makes it clear that the visit there described had two main features: (a) a discussion of the Gentile mission and the terms on which it could be regarded as legitimate, and (b) a request that Paul should remember the poor, 'which very thing,' he says, 'I was (*or* had been) eager to do.' In Acts 11, 12 Luke describes a visit the purpose of which was to bring relief to those suffering from famine; in Acts 15 he describes a visit when the legitimacy and basis of the Gentile mission were discussed. It is no far-fetched hypothesis that one of his sources (there is no need here to discuss the question whether his sources were written or oral) told him of a famine visit, another of a theological discussion of the missionary situation, and that he wrongly supposed that these sources referred to different occasions. This hypothesis leaves us with questions about the chronology of Acts and especially the relation of the 'first missionary journey' to the Council; I hope to discuss these elsewhere. What stands firm is the identification of Galatians 2 with Acts 15, which further consideration makes even stronger than Lightfoot's argument.

12 At Galatians 2.4f. the majority of MSS contain the following text: (a) 'But on account of (διὰ δέ) false brothers, privily brought in, who crept in to spy out our liberty which we have in Christ Jesus, in order that they might enslave us, to whom not even for a moment did we yield in subjection, in order that the truth of the gospel might continue with (*or* for) you.'

A few MSS and fathers (D* b; Ir^lat Tert MVict Ambst Hier^ms) omit 'to whom not even' (οἷς οὐδέ). This gives the text: (b) 'But on account of false brothers ... we yielded in subjection for a moment, in order that the truth of the gospel might continue with [*or* for] you.'

There is a small quantity of evidence which suggests that there may have been a text (beginning in v. 3) that ran: (c) 'Titus was not compelled to be circumcised on account of false brothers [omitting δέ] ... In order that they might not enslave us, we yielded in subjection for a moment ...'

Text (a) is grammatically defective; it lacks a main verb. Text (b) is grammatically complete, and represents Paul as making a tactical submission: Yield now in order to hold firm later. Text (c) can hardly be right; it has to be pressed to give the sense of my translation. We have to choose between the imperfect construction of (a) and the curious tactics of (b); and to do so bearing in mind the fact that (b) appears in only one Greek MS (subsequently corrected) and one Latin MS. Paul was not a careful writer; he did on occasion write sentences which it is impossible to construe in accordance with the rules of Greek grammar. The whole of Galatians 2, indeed the whole of the epistle, expresses an adamant refusal to compromise on the issue of circumcision. It seems very much more probable that Paul wrote (or his amanuensis took down) a piece of bad Greek than that he gave way in the test case of the Gentile Titus. How is it that reading (b) appears in a number of early fathers? It probably reached them through the Old Latin VS, and, when known, was valued because it contradicted Marcion (so at least Tertullian). Paul then almost certainly wrote the text in form (a). His incomplete sentence may have been due simply to inadvertence. Some think it was due to embarrassment; hence suggestions alluded to in the text: Titus was not *compelled* to be circumcised, but was circumcised; Titus had himself circumcised against Paul's will.

13 This is probably how they spoke of themselves. See pp. 80, 81.

14 Cf. 2.10, where the word *only* (μόνον) is significant; that was all they asked.

15 See pp. 7, 8.

16 Baur, F. C., *Paulus* (Stuttgart 1845), p. 125; (2nd edn 1866), pp. 142f. Baur's understanding of early Christian history, and especially of Paul's place within it, though open at some points to correction,

retains very high value, and must not be lightly written off.

17 See also pp. 81, 84–6. Galatians will serve very well as a tract for our own times.

18 An interesting negative glimpse of Paul's theologically determined behaviour is given by 1.10. He neither persuades men by pleasing (flattering) them, nor persuades God, as does a magician, by harnessing divine forces for his own ends. His actions are governed (he claims) by the truth.

19 See the literature cited by Betz, op. cit., p. 113.

20 Peter's action is hypocrisy in that it is the attitude of a Mr Facing-both-ways. See 'Apostles in Council and in Conflict', pp. 100–2.

21 E. P. Sanders (in *Paul and Palestinian Judaism*, London 1977) has emphasized the gracious initiative of God in establishing the covenant and making it available to the Jewish people. Entering into the covenant carried with it the obligation to obey (pp. 93–103). For parallels between Sanders' exposition of Judaism and the theology of the Judaizers, see pp. 32, 34.

22 The Hebrew is less explicit.

23 For this exegetical method and Paul's use of it in Romans 4 see my commentary, pp. 89f.

24 The Hebrew may be understood not as a passive ('they shall be blessed') but as a reflexive ('they shall bless themselves'), that is, when wishing themselves well they will say, 'May we be as fortunate as Abraham.'

25 It is of 3.20 that Lightfoot wrote, 'The number of interpretations of this verse is said to mount up to 250 or 300. Many of these arise out of an error as to the mediator, many more disregard the context, and not a few are quite arbitrary.' Lightfoot takes the sense to be that the existence of a mediator implies the presence of two parties, God who commands and the people who must obey. But in this sense a promise requires the presence of two parties as much as does a law, and the contrast Paul is making disappears. It is better to take the verse as in the text.

26 I have discussed the interpretation of the 'allegory' more fully in *Rechtfertigung, Festschrift für Ernst Käsemann* (Tübingen & Göttingen 1976), pp. 1–16.

27 It may be that we should compare 6.16, the Israel of God. But see Hebrews 12.22; Revelation 21.2.

28 Bligh, John, *Galatians,* Householder Commentaries No 1 (London 1969), pp. 18, 91, 235, 391, 407. Cf. Betz ad loc.

29 For Paul's use of Spirit see pp. 74. Readers of the epistle in Greek will note in 3.14 two ἵνα (final) clauses. They should be taken as parallel, equally dependent on the main verb ἐξηγόρασεν in v. 13.

In addition to the fact that the 'promise of the Spirit' is a good definition of the blessing of Abraham, διὰ τῆς πίστεως in the second clause is precisely the means by which the blessing of Abraham is received.

30 See note 21.

31 The outstanding feature of Betz's commentary (note 1) is his use of Greek controversial literature to illustrate the form and argument of Galatians. Even if (as may be) he has to some extent exaggerated the relation between the epistle and Greek rhetoric, his analysis, and the parallels that he draws, are most illuminating.

32 εἰς χριστόν, sometimes taken to mean that the παιδαγωγός (the law) was intended to lead us to (the school of) Christ. The temporal meaning of εἰς is however much more probable here; the thought of the paragraph is that if the law *led* anywhere it led to prison (v. 23).

33 The argument turns to some extent on 1 Corinthians 7 and 11, on which see the notes in my commentary (London 1968).

34 Sherwin-White, A. N., *Racial Prejudice in Imperial Rome* (Cambridge 1970), pp. 99f.

35 If Paul had had 'body' (σῶμα) in mind he would have used the neuter of the numeral, ἕν. εἷς implies a masculine noun, and the only one available in the context is υἱός, 'son'.

36 It seems to be impossible to trace the myth of the descending and ascending redeemer in pre-Christian literature. This does not prove that it did not exist in pre-Christian times, but it is virtually certain that if it did so exist it must have been given infinitely greater definiteness by the belief that a known historical person, Jesus of Nazareth, was a divine person who had descended from heaven and returned thither. Philippians 2 plays a part in this process.

37 It would lead too far from the main theme of this book if we were to discuss the relation between the law of destiny as understood by astrologers and gnostics, the law of Moses, and natural law – if indeed we were to attempt to reach a definition of natural law and to relate it to Paul's theology. He undoubtedly had a conception of nature (φύσις) and of conscience (συνείδησις) which in some respects recalls Stoic ideas, though he uses these ideas in a way completely different from the Stoics. There is however a profitable field of inquiry here, and the relation between freedom and obligation that Paul will work out in terms of the divine act of revelation and redemption in Christ is one that can be applied in any department of human life.

38 Galatians 4.5, like 3.14 (see note 29), contains two ἵνα clauses. These also are parallel in that both are dependent on ἐξαπέστειλεν, yet the second is epexegetic of the first in the way pointed out in the text.

39 For the use of '*Abba*' see especially Jeremias, J., *New Testament Theology* I (London 1971) pp. 61–8; or better, *Abba* (Göttingen 1966) pp. 15–67. Jeremias may perhaps overpress his case a little, but it is as good as certain that '*Abba*' was not in normal liturgical use, and was in use in the family circle.

40 That thought of a gnostic kind was current at the time the New Testament was written seems clear; whether anything that can be called developed gnosticism was current at that time is another question. See Wilson, R. McL., *Gnosis and the New Testament*, Oxford 1968.

41 The opening verse, 4.12, is very obscure. See Betz (note 1). If Paul is not simply appealing to the mutual understanding that ought to exist between friends his meaning will probably be: 'Become as I am, share my attitude to the law and especially its ceremonial ordinances; for I, Jew that I am, have come to share your Gentile life.'

42 Paul speaks of the way he was received when he preached in Galatia τὸ πρότερον. Strictly this should mean, 'On the former of two occasions,' and it has been used in dating the epistle and locating Galatia. It is however unwise to lay so much stress on a rigid interpretation of τὸ πρότερον, which may be used to mean no more than 'At the beginning' or 'The first time'. You received me, Paul says, as an angel of God, as Christ Jesus himself. He moves along an ascending scale. Christ Jesus is higher than an angel; there is no 'angel Christology' here.

43 See note 21. The question at issue at this point in Galatians could be expressed thus: Given that the initial act of God in electing and delivering Israel is an act of grace, is grace neutralized and overthrown when (430 years later, in Paul's chronology) the law is added to the promise? In other words, in the term 'convenantal nomism', is there a contradiction between the adjective and the noun? If there is, does the adjective outweigh the noun or the noun the adjective?

44 Daube, D., *The New Testament and Rabbinic Judaism* (London 1956) p. 278.

45 Käsemann, E., 'Gottesgerechtigkeit bei Paulus', *Exegetische Versuche und Besinnungen II* (Göttingen 1964), pp. 181–93; Stuhlmacher, P., *Gerechtigkeit Gottes bei Paulus*. Göttingen 1965.

46 E.g. Schweitzer, A., *The Mysticism of Paul the Apostle*. London 1931; Stendahl, K., *Paul among Jews and Gentiles*. London 1977.

47 See note 31.

48 See note 5.

49 See Deissmann, A., *Light from the Ancient East* (London 1911) pp. 324–34. Betz (op. cit., p. 258) rightly points out that at Galatians 5.1 the language used by Paul 'does not include the terms of purchase, purchase price, or "slave of Christ".' To some extent however these may be supplied from the use of ἐξαγοράζειν at 3.13; 4.5.

50 'There are two dangers threatening the Christian freedom of the Galatians: (1) the acceptance of the Jewish Torah (5.2–12), and (2) the corruption of their life by the "flesh" (5.13–24)' (op. cit., p. 258).

51 Ropes, J. H., *The Singular Problem of the Epistle to the Galatians*. Cambridge (Mass.) 1929.

52 Lütgert, W., *Gesetz und Geist*, Beiträge zur Förderung Christlicher Theologie 22.6. Gütersloh 1919.

53 Munck, J., *Paulus und die Heilsgeschichte* (Copenhagen 1954), pp. 79–126.

54 Schmithals, W., *Paulus und die Gnostiker* (Hamburg-Bergstedt 1965), pp. 9–46.

55 Bligh, J., see note 28.

56 I quote the translation of G. Vermes, *The Dead Sea Scrolls in English*. Harmondsworth 1962.

57 See note 16.

58 Käsemann, E., 'Die Legitimität des Apostels', *Zeitschrift für die Neutestamentliche Wissenschaft* 41 (1942), pp. 33–71; reprinted Darmstadt 1956.

59 The participle ἐνεργουμένη may be either middle (faith *working* through love) or passive (faith *being worked out, activated,* through love). Pauline usage is decisively in favour of the former. As Lightfoot says, 'this passage does not express the doctrine of "*fides caritate formata*".'

60 On the rendering of 2.6 (*not* 'what they once were . . .') and its significance, see Aland, K., 'Wann starb Petrus?', *New Testament Studies* 2 (1956), pp. 267–75.

61 See 'Apostles in Council and in Conflict', pp. 98–102.

62 See especially von Campenhausen, H., 'Ein Witz des Apostels Paulus', *Neutestamentliche Studien für Rudolf Bultmann* (Berlin 1954), pp. 189–93. Von Campenhausen speaks of the verse as '*einen in jeder Hinsicht "blutigen" Witz*' (p. 190); but Paul was not thinking seriously in terms of a literal fulfilment of his wish.

63 So e.g. Hillel; cf. Aqiba and ben Azzai (Strack-Billerbeck i. 357–9).

64 Davies, W. D., 'Paul and the Dead Sea Scrolls: Flesh and Spirit'. *The Scrolls and the New Testament* Stendahl, K., ed. (London 1958), pp. 157–82.

65 W. Shakespeare, *King Richard III*, Act 5, Scene 3.

66 There are textural problems in 6.9, 10. In 6.9 many MSS read not the verb ἐγκακεῖν, to neglect one's duty, but ἐκκακεῖν, to grow weary (cf. 2 Corinthians 4.1, 16, where the same variation occurs). There can be little doubt that Paul was urging his readers to do what was their plain duty. In 6.10 some MSS have the indicative ἔχομεν, 'now that we have opportunity', others the subjunctive ἔχωμεν, 'as long as we have opportunity'. The variation makes little difference to the general sense.

67 Op. cit., p. 486.

68 It is impossible to answer the purely grammatical question whether the antecedent of the relative οὗ is χριστός or σταυρός. If it is 'Christ', it is Christ crucified; if it is 'cross', it is cross as standing for Christ crucified.

69 See Bultmann, R., *Theologie des Neuen Testaments* 8th edn (Tübingen 1980), especially pp. 315–53.

70 For the word κανών see 2 Corinthians 10.12–18, with the notes in my commentary (London 1973).

71 Haenchen, E., *Die Apostelgeschichte* (Göttingen 1977), p. 121.

72 See note 16.

73 Braun, H., *Gesammelte Studien* (Tübingen 1962), p. 324.

74 Kümmel, W. G., *Einleitung in das Neue Testament* (Heidelberg 1978), p. 450; the whole context should be consulted.

75 Boehmer, H., *Der junge Luther* (Gotha 1951), pp. 127f.

76 Holl, K., *Gesammelte Aufsätze zur Kirchengeschichte* (Tübingen 1921), 1. pp. 430f.

77 Barth, K., *The Knowledge of God and the Service of God* (London 1938), p. 179 – but Barth says this everywhere, e.g. *Evangelical Theology* (London 1963), p. 43; *Church Dogmatics* I 1 (ET, Edinburgh 1936), p. 51.

Index of Biblical and Other Passages

Index of Names and Subjects